THE RIGHT
TO LIVE;
THE RIGHT
TO DIE

THE RIGHT TO LIVE; THE RIGHT TO DIE

C. Everett Koop M.D., Sc.D.

 TYNDALE HOUSE PUBLISHERS, INC.
Wheaton, Illinois

COVERDALE HOUSE PUBLISHERS, LTD.
Eastbourne, England

Library of Congress Catalog Card Number 76-8682. ISBN 0-8423-5593-6, paper. Copyright © 1976 by Tyndale House Publishers, Inc., Wheaton, Illinois. All rights reserved. Third printing, September 1976. Printed in the United States of America.

To my wife
Betty
with whom I have shared
all my problems
and who has unselfishly
shared me with them
in return.

"For my part I believe that there is no life so degraded, debased, deteriorated or impoverished that it does not deserve respect and is not worth defending with zeal and conviction ... Above all I believe that a terrible precedent would be established if we agreed that a life could be allowed to end because it is not worth preserving since the notion of biological worthiness, even if carefully circumscribed at first, would soon become broader and less precise. After eliminating what was no longer human, the next step would be to eliminate what was not sufficiently human, and finally nothing would be spared except what fitted a certain ideal concept of humanity.

"I have the weakness to believe that it is an honor for a society to desire the expensive luxury of sustaining life for its useless, incompetent, and incurably ill members. I would almost measure society's degree of civilization by the amount of effort and vigilance it imposes on itself out of pure respect for life. It is noble to struggle unrelentingly to save someone's life as if he were dear to us, when objectively he has no value and is not even loved by anyone."

Jean Rostan, French biologist,
from his book, Humanly Possible,
translated by the Saturday Review Press

CONTENTS

FOREWORD

The highest level of moral culture is that at which the people of a nation recognize and protect the sanctity of innocent human life. Since the dawn of civilization, all great nations in which freedom and justice have governed the affairs of the people have upheld this principle, giving it the highest priority in their laws and customs. Indeed, this principle is the bedrock of Western civilization—the one principle, above all others, which has distinguished free and democratic systems from the barbaric regimes of the past and the totalitarian systems of today.

It is for this reason that abortion—the taking of innocent human life—has, until very recent times, been viewed as violative of the Judeo-Christian tradition of the free world, and prohibited by law. And it is no mere coincidence that the modern practice of abortion first appeared as a policy of government in the communist dictatorships, where contempt for the dignity of human life is widely demonstrated.

Two hundred years ago, a great nation was founded on principles of human rights—the right to life, liberty, and the pursuit of happiness. These are the lofty principles which appear in one of the most important documents in history, the Declaration of Independence of the United States of America. Three years ago, a dark shadow was cast over this document when the highest tribunal in the land, the Supreme Court, ruled that an unborn child in the womb is not a person entitled to the right to life, and may be deprived of

11

life by the mother and her attending physician. The decision has thrown America into a moral crisis that can only be regarded as a cause for rejoicing among her adversaries.

There comes a time in the history of all great civilizations when the moral foundations upon which it rests are shaken by some momentous turn of events. That time has come for America. The historical experience of Western man indicates that such upheavals can ultimately destroy a nation—the collapse of Rome being only one of many examples. Great nations die when they cease to live by the great principles which gave them the vision and strength to rise above tyranny and human degradation. Unless the abortion decision is reversed by an amendment to the Constitution, the future of America is in grave doubt, for no nation can remain free or exercise moral leadership when it has embraced the doctrine of death.

Whether we survive the present crisis or succumb to the moral irresponsibility of the Supreme Court depends in large measure on our ability as a people to re-educate ourselves in those first principles which gave us the life, the liberty, and the pursuit of happiness that have now been eclipsed. As an informed people, we have the power to overcome ignorance and restore the right-to-life to our fundamental law. In this important book, Dr. C. Everett Koop has provided us with the torch of learning and wisdom that can show us the way back home. Every American, whatever his beliefs, will learn much from Dr. Koop's keen insights and profound understanding.

Jesse Helms
U. S. Senator

PREFACE

My interest in the sanctity of human life had its beginnings with Douglas Jackson, a surgeon of renown in England and a Christian gentleman of broad understanding and profound faith. As I began to express my own feelings concerning the sanctity of human life in discussions with medical students, interns, and residents, or in seminars on personal ethics with college students, I came to a position concerning abortion with which I was comfortable. Stated briefly it was that I was fundamentally and basically opposed to abortion but there was a time when my Christian compassion crossed this Christian absolute and there was room for abortion in "hard" cases.

Several years back, at about the time that some of the states liberalized their abortion laws, I spoke several times in a matter of a few days to different groups in Fresno, California, on the subject of the sanctity of human life. On each of these occasions, where possible, I drew a horizontal line on the blackboard and indicated that that was my absolute prohibition against abortion. Toward the right termination of that line a diagonal crossed it and this was my Christian compassion; there was room in certain circumstances for an abortion.

The last of the occasions I had to speak during those days was to the combined chapel service of the Pacific Mennonite College and Seminary. A former Philadelphian, a registered nurse working in Fresno, drove me to my final speaking engagement. En route we were discussing what she had heard me say on the sanctity of life the previous evening before a different audience. Just before we arrived at our destination she said something like this: "I've always been against abortion but I knew that if my daughter were raped and became pregnant she would have an abortion. However, since I've been working here in a hospital where day after day unborn babies are killed by abortion I have decided that if my daughter were raped and if she did become pregnant she would carry it through. I would consider that to be just as much in the sovereignty of God as anything else that touched our lives."

Whether it was that statement, or whether it was the slow pressure of what I had read in the Scriptures concerning the sanctity of life, I do not know, but when at the following chapel service I came to the point of drawing my two lines, I abandoned my notes and said: "My position on abortion is essentially Roman Catholic but for different reasons."

As more and more people began to talk about the need for liberalized abortion laws, and as I saw the public being deliberately misled by statistics on deaths from criminal abortions, I felt compelled to take a stand for the sanctity of human life. I did this without being a member of any organized group; indeed, my association with any pro-life movement has been in the very recent past. When the Supreme Court decided in January 1973 that the unborn child had absolutely no rights, I saw this as the herald of a number of other things that would erode the morality of this society. I became convinced that the Supreme Court decision would open the door for a number of things that even those in favor of abortion on demand would not want to buy in one package along with abortion.

In a commencement address delivered to the graduating class at Wheaton College in Illinois in 1973, I pointed out ten things that I thought were likely to happen because of the

Supreme Court's decision. As they happened one by one I realized that my concerns were well founded and that the other end of the life span would soon be the target for legislation.

When the Karen Quinlan case became international news I was very much concerned that the relationship of a physician with his dying patient would become a legal matter. When Judge Robert Muir, Jr., decided that our Constitution provides no right to die, the editorial comment in many quarters called for legislation to take care of the Karen Quinlans of the future. The dangers from such a course of action for you and me are far greater than those following the decision for abortion on demand. I felt that it was time to put into writing my thoughts on the right to live and the right to die.

Although they are probably unaware of it, Harold O. J. Brown and Carl Henry, both theologians, and Jay MacMoran, a medical doctor, provided encouragement for me to do this. My wife, Betty, was helpful in every conceivable way and kept my doctrine straight. Robert Grasberger and Jeffrey Janoski were helpful in finding legal references, as was David Knighton in the medical field. Louise Schnaufer and Betty Smith filled in a lot of holes in my professional life while I was working on the manuscript. The typing and retyping was accomplished by Eiko Ikeda for The Right to Live and by Ruth Davenport for The Right to Die. To all of these, and to the students, residents, and interns I have used for a sounding board, I am very grateful.

INTRODUCTION

We are a schizophrenic society. We will fly a deformed newborn baby four hundred miles by airplane to perform a series of remarkable operations on such a youngster, knowing full well that the end result will be far less than perfect. We will ship food to a starving nation overseas, and, at the same time, supply arms to its enemy. We will feed another starving people beset by famine, but we will make no attempt to ask them to try to control their population by contraception. We will stop a cholera epidemic by vaccine in a country unable to feed itself, so that the people can survive cholera in order to die of starvation. While we struggle to save the life of a three-pound baby in a hospital's newborn intensive care unit, obstetricians in the same hospital are destroying similar infants yet unborn.

So it is not unpredictable that in this society we should be considering the pros and the cons of abortion and euthanasia.

In presenting these subjects in the broader sense of the right to live and the right to die, it will be assumed that the reader knows bits and pieces of these matters but that he will bear with me if I start at square one. It is my intention to tell you of my own credentials to speak on this subject, to give some background on abortion, to describe the development of an unborn baby, and to describe briefly the several techniques for performing an abortion. Then we will review what the current situation is legally, what this means in practice, and then recount the arguments you will hear in favor of abortion. Then, I would like to assume the role of prophet and outline for you the implications of the Supreme Court's decision on abortion in reference to the future of this country and in reference to your life and mine as well as the lives of our children. Finally, I would like to look at the end of life with you and discuss the subject you hear of and read about as the "right to die" and "death with dignity."

Professionally, I do not speak on this subject in a vacuum. For more than a quarter of a century I have been engaged in the surgical care of children and perhaps that for which I am best known professionally is the operative approach to newborn babies who are born with defects which are incompatible with life, but nevertheless can be corrected by the proper surgery at the proper time. These are youngsters who are born without a rectum, or have no esophagus with which to swallow, or have their abdominal organs out in the umbilical cord, or have their abdominal organs up in the chest, or have one of many varieties of intestinal obstruction. Each one of these defects is correctable. Many of them take years of rehabilitation before a youngster is able to return to society, and some of these children, in spite of all that we do for them, are never what society calls normal.

I could not have taken care of hundreds of these babies and their families without seeing the joy and the triumph of a life saved, but also the heartbreak of a surgical success somewhat less than perfect. I know the economic burden on the family; I know the problem of chronic illness for the family, for the child, and for the community. I know the psychological burden on such a youngster as he grows up, as well as the problems that the family has to face as he goes to school, encounters new friends, and tries to achieve a position in the community socially and economically.

One can really only speak on an issue such as this from the place where he stands. To know why a person reacts as he does to a given situation would require knowing all of his upbringing and life experience up until that time. As man matures, his judgments on ethical issues are based upon some deep-seated absolutes to which are added precepts based upon experience. In the culture which is Judeo-Christian, for many individuals the basis of decision comes from one's understanding of God. However, even for those who disclaim any interest in God there exists a bias for life which is a spinoff of the Judeo-Christian heritage.

I speak as a Christian. I am an evangelical who believes that Jesus Christ was who he said he was and that he came to do what he said he came to do. Jesus Christ said he was the unique Son of God and that he came into the world to save sinners. This is good news, this is what men call the gospel, and this is what I believe. As a Christian I have the supreme court to which I take my problems for appeal and settlement, and that is the Word of God, the Bible. Just as Jesus Christ made claims about himself, the Bible makes claims about itself. It claims to be the Word of God and to be profitable for doctrine, for reproof, for correction, and for instruction in righteousness.[1] This I believe, as well as the divine inspiration and the infallibility of Scripture.

ONE
THE RIGHT TO LIVE

The whole question of the right to live presents anyone who considers it with a number of dilemmas; I have lived through many of them. Let me give you an example: I could have a telephone call any day from an outlying hospital saying that they had just delivered a baby who has no rectum, whose bladder is inside out, whose abdominal organs are out in his umbilical cord, and who has a cleft spine with an opening in his back so that you can see his spinal cord. In addition, his legs are in such a position that his feet lie most comfortably next to his ears. Now, every one of those defects is correctable. But think of the cost! I am not simply talking about money, but think of the cost in anxiety for the family, for the hospital staff, for me; think of the emotional drain on all the people concerned; think of the emotional problems for that youngster in the six or seven years it will take before he is corrected.* Now the dilemma that is presented to some people in such a situation is this: "Should we operate or should we not? Should we let this baby die, unattended, or should we do the things that we know how to do best and let him live?"

*I treated a boy who had half of these things plus a few others. He has had more than twenty-five operations. I see him and his family in the community about once a week. They are a great family and consider the boy and his problems to be the best experience life has offered them. The boy is a delight. He has strengthened the family and has taught them compassion and understanding.

Dilemma is defined as "a perplexing predicament, a necessary choice between two equally undesirable alternatives." I am not sure that everyone would agree that the two alternatives I have mentioned are equally undesirable. Yet, everyone talks about rights these days and I would like you to consider whether you think this baby has the right to live. Does this family have the right of a choice? Do I, as the baby's surgeon, have a right of choice? Do I have the right or the privilege to try to influence the family to think the way I do?

In 1776, in Philadelphia, Thomas Jefferson said, "We hold these truths to be self-evident, that all men are created equal, they are endowed with certain inalienable rights; among these are life, liberty and the pursuit of happiness."[1] Now think about that for a moment. Think about the baby's right to life. Think about the family's right to happiness. Think about my right to the liberty of choice, and think about the baby's right to all of those things.

When I write of the right to live, I acknowledge at the outset that God is the Author and the Giver of life and that you and I as his servants have no right to destroy it. I am speaking of human life, not animal life, and I am not speaking of that perverted doctrine of Albert Schweitzer of the reverence *for* life,[2] where he afforded the same reverence for life to the termites eating away the foundations of his hospital as he did the patients in the hospital endangered by the termites.

The Bible tells us that man was made in the image of God and at least one meaning of that statement is that, like God, each of us is a trinity. I am a soul, I inhabit a body, and I have a spirit. Everything I read in the Word of God tells me that my soul is immortal and, like it or not, you and I will be conscious beings throughout all eternity.

We are not the first society to wonder about these things. Primitive societies before the Greeks and the Romans practiced infanticide. This is how they controlled their population, and took care of their food problem and their economics. The Greeks, a people who command such respect in philosophical circles, believed that society should get rid of the frail and the deformed and the aged. This was the belief of Plutarch, Plato, and Aristotle.[3] The Romans considered that slaughter was a triumph and that infanticide was a prudent form of household economy. Even so, those ancient cultures saw abortion as killing.[4] The New Testament does not specifically proscribe abortion. It is silent on the matter. However, Christian writings from the first part of the second century, according to Harold O. J. Brown,[5] give this exposition of the commandment, "Thou shalt love thy neighbor as thyself": "Thou shalt do no murder; thou shalt not commit adultery; thou shalt not commit sodomy; thou shalt not commit fornication; thou shalt not steal; thou shalt not use magic; thou shalt not use filturers; thou shalt not procure abortion or commit infanticide; thou shalt not covet thy neighbor's goods."

ORIGIN OF THE SANCTITY OF LIFE

The sanctity of human life begins, as I see it, with the various covenants between God and man. The first of these was after Abel had been killed by Cain and Cain was cursed by God. God was very careful to point out that there was to be no blood feud and if there were, his punishment would take place sevenfold.[6] After the flood, God spoke to Noah and told him that whoever sheds man's blood, by man shall that individual's blood be shed.[7] Many believe that was the mandate from God for capital punishment. After that came the Ten Commandments, and one of those was, "Thou shalt not kill."[8] It is very clear from the context that the commandment, "Thou shalt not kill," had nothing to do with capital punishment or with manslaughter, or with war, but it had to do with murder.[9] All of these covenants, if you read them carefully, were based upon one thing; man's uniqueness in having been created in the image of God.

It was soon obvious in Judaism that life was precious to God. Christian doctrine is based upon Judaism, plus the teachings of Jesus and the apostles as recorded in the New Testament. Jesus claimed that his teachings were in harmony with the teachings of the Old Testament.[10] He said further that the moral law was immutable and unchanging. He showed how learned men, such as the Pharisees, could misinterpret the law.[11] In the final analysis, as a Christian, I believe in the sanctity of life because I am God's by creation and also God's by redemption through Jesus Christ and his sacrifice on the cross in my behalf.

LOGICAL AND THEOLOGICAL ARGUMENTS

The liberalization of abortion laws has brought the whole problem of the sanctity of life into focus. My reasons against abortion are logical as well as theological.

First, the logic. It is impossible for anyone to say when a developing fetus or embryo or baby becomes viable, that is, has the ability to exist on its own. The logical approach is to go back to the sperm and the egg. A sperm has twenty-three chromosomes and no matter what, even though it is alive and can fertilize an egg, it can never make another sperm. An egg also has twenty-three chromosomes and it can never make another egg. So, we have eggs that cannot reproduce and we have sperm that cannot reproduce unless they get together. Once there is the union of sperm and egg, and the twenty-three chromosomes of each are brought together into one cell that has forty-six chromosomes, we have an entirely different story. That one cell with its forty-six chromosomes has all of the DNA (desoxyribonucleic acid), the whole genetic code, that will, if not interrupted, make a human being just like you, with the potential for God-consciousness. I do not know anyone among my medical confreres, no matter how pro-abortion he might be, who would kill a newborn baby the minute he was born. (He might let him starve to death. He would not kill him.)[12,13] My question to my pro-abortion friend who will not kill a newborn baby is this: "Would you kill this infant a minute before he was born, or a minute before that, or a minute before that, or a minute before that?" You see what I am getting at. At what minute can one consider life to be worthless and the next minute consider that same life to be precious? So much for logic.

Although there are ample reasons for the areligious individual to be frightened about the implications of the Supreme Court's decision on abortion, I do believe that most anti-abortion individuals lean heavily upon religious convictions in coming to their pro-life position. The basis of belief may be far away in time and vague in detail but nevertheless has built into the conscience a judgment concerning right and wrong. Although I am not a theologian, I feel you should know how I have come theologically to the position I now hold. Two of the Christian doctrines which I cherish most are the sovereignty of God and the infallibility of Scripture. By sovereignty I mean that even though God has apparently given man free will, that free will is nevertheless within the sovereignty of God. How could it be otherwise if God is God? God is accountable to no one for his decisions. Even the breath that men use to blaspheme God is a gift from God himself. As I read the Scriptures, they seem to say from cover to cover that life is precious to God. I can find no place in the Bible which clearly states when a fetus might be viable but there are some passages which are extremely significant.

In the 139th Psalm, David writing about himself says, "Yea, the darkness hideth not from thee; but the night shineth as the day: the darkness and the light are both alike to thee. For thou hast possessed my inner parts: thou hast covered me in my mother's womb. I will praise thee; for I am fearfully and wonderfully made: marvellous are thy works; and that my soul knoweth right well. My substance was not hid from thee, when I was made in secret, and curiously wrought in the lowest parts of the earth. Thine eyes did see my substance, yet being unperfect; and in thy book all my members were written, which in continuance were fashioned, when as yet there was none of them."[14]

I am also impressed that when the Bible speaks of man in the womb, it also speaks of the whole sweep of the creation and of God's sovereignty from then until the end of time. In the 44th chapter of Isaiah we read, "Yet now hear, O Jacob my servant; and Israel, whom I have chosen: Thus saith the Lord that made thee, and formed thee from the womb, which will help thee."[15] And then the prophet goes on to quote Jehovah in reference to the creation, the pouring out of his spirit, his blessing upon Israel, the forgiveness of their transgressions, and then he goes on to say, "Thus saith the Lord, thy redeemer, and he who formed thee from the womb, I am the Lord that maketh all things; that stretcheth forth the heavens alone; that spreadeth abroad the earth by myself."[16] When God called Jeremiah to be a prophet, he said this: "Before I formed thee in the belly I knew thee; before thou camest forth out of the womb, I sanctified thee..."[17]

I believe this refutes any question about a later viability of the fetus and it certainly supports the New Testament doctrine that God knew us from before the foundation of the world. Now many people will agree with these passages, but they will say, "What about the deformed baby: Don't tell me you mean the same thing about a baby who was born with some kind of a defect!" Well, God has an answer to that. You will remember that when God called Moses to serve him in Egypt, he met him at the burning bush[18] and he said that he wanted him to go and speak to Pharaoh and after that, he would have Pharaoh let his people, Israel, go. Moses did not like that idea at all, and he protested to the Lord, "I am not eloquent, neither heretofore nor since Thou hast spoken unto Thy servant, but I am slow of speech and of a slow tongue."[19] God answered Moses, "Who hath made man's mouth or who maketh the dumb or the deaf or the seeing or the blind? Have not I, saith the Lord?"[20] So, it seems to me that whether you like it or not, God makes what we call the perfect and the imperfect. This is a hard doctrine to accept but I think one has to agree that if God is God, if God is sovereign, then he is not able to make a mistake.

DEVELOPMENT BEFORE BIRTH

Having already mentioned the union of sperm and egg to give forty-six chromosomes, let us briefly review the development of a baby. By the time a baby is eighteen to twenty-five days old, long before the mother is sure that she is pregnant, the heart is already beating. At forty-five days after conception, you can pick up electroencephalographic waves from the baby's developing brain. At eight weeks, there is not only a brain, but the fingerprints on the hands have already formed and except for size, will never change. By the ninth and tenth weeks, the thyroid and the adrenal glands are functioning. The baby can squint, swallow, move his tongue and the sex hormones are already present. By twelve and thirteen weeks, he has fingernails, he sucks his thumb and he can recoil from pain. In the fourth month the growing baby is eight to ten inches in height. In the fifth month there is a time of lengthening and strengthening of the developing infant. Skin, hair, and nails grow. Sweat glands arise. Oil glands excrete. This is the month in which the movements of the infant are felt by his mother. It has always seemed extraordinary to me that as the pregnant woman feels the first movements within the uterus, the mother-to-be says, "Today I felt life." In the sixth month the developing baby responds to light and to sound. He can sleep and awake. He gets hiccups and can hear the beat of his mother's heart. Survival outside the womb is now possible. In the seventh month the nervous system becomes much more complex, the infant is sixteen inches long and weighs about three pounds. In the final eighth and ninth months there is a time of fattening and of continued growth.[21]

TECHNIQUES OF ABORTION

There are three commonly used techniques of abortion; each may have its variations. The technique that is used most commonly for early pregnancies is called the D & C, or dilation and curettage. In this technique, which is carried out between the seventh and twelfth weeks of pregnancy, the uterus is approached through the vagina. The cervix is stretched to permit the insertion of instruments. The surgeon then scrapes the wall of the uterus, cutting the baby's body to pieces and scraping the placenta from its attachments on the uterine wall. Bleeding is considerable.[22] An alternate method to be used at the same time is called suction abortion. The principle is the same as the D & C. More than 66 percent of all abortions performed in the United States and Canada are done by this method.[23] A powerful suction tube is inserted through the open cervix. This tears apart the body of the developing baby and his placenta, sucking them into a jar. These smaller parts of the body are recognizable as arms, legs, head, etc.

Later in pregnancy, when the D & C or suction abortion might produce too great a hemorrhage on the part of the mother, the second most common type of abortion comes into being. This is called the salt poisoning abortion, or "salting out." This method is carried out after sixteen weeks of pregnancy, when enough fluid has accumulated in the sac around the baby. A rather long needle is inserted through the mother's abdomen directly into the sac surrounding the baby and a solution of concentrated salt is injected into it. The baby breathes in and swallows the salt and is poisoned by it. There are changes in osmotic pressure; the outer layer of skin is burned off by the high concentration of the salt; brain hemorrhages are frequent. It takes about an hour to slowly kill the baby by this method. The mother usually goes into labor about a day later and delivers a dead, shriveled baby.[24]

If abortion is decided upon too late to be accomplished by either the D & C or salting out procedures, there is left a final technique of abortion called hysterotomy. A hysterotomy is exactly the same as a cesarean section with the one difference, namely, that in a cesarean section the operation is being done to save the life of the baby whereas in the hysterotomy the operation is being done to kill the baby.[25] These babies look very much like other babies except that they are small, weighing, for example, about two pounds at the end of a twenty-four-week pregnancy. These babies are truly alive and they are allowed to die through neglect or are deliberately killed by a variety of methods.

Hysterotomy gives the fetus the best chance, but at a very high price in morbidity and a risk of mortality for the mother fifteen times greater than that of saline infusion, the more commonly used alternative.[26] A Boston jury found a physician guilty of manslaughter for killing the product of this type of abortion.*[27]

That children are really born alive in abortion performed by hysterotomy is a fact. In *Markle* versus *Able,* in the Supreme Court of the United States,[28] there is a table listing twenty-seven live births after abortions. Babies delivered by hysterotomy with the intent of abortion are obviously sources of concern to abortionists. In the collected letters of the Internation Correspondence Society of Obstetricians and Gynecologists (November 1, 1974) the question was how obstetricians handle live births in abortions. A Philadelphia physician wrote: "At the time of delivery it has been our policy to wrap the fetus in a towel. The fetus is then moved to another room, while our attention is turned to the care of the gravida (former mother-to-be). She is examined to determine whether placental expulsion has occurred and the extent of vaginal bleeding. Once we are sure her condition is stable, the fetus is evaluated. Almost invariably all signs of life have ceased."[29]

BEFORE THE SUPREME COURT'S DECISION RE ABORTION

As recently as 1962, an Arizona housewife took Thalidomide, which she had obtained in Europe previously. When the story of limbless children, produced by Thalidomide ingestion in pregnant women, became a medical fact in Germany, the Arizona woman, now an expectant

---

*In New York City in 1957-1959, 28-week live-born infants had 60 percent probability of survival. In 1966-1970 in Montreal, such infants had a 92.2 percent chance of surviving the first week after birth. The 1973 maternal death rate for amniotic fluid exchange (saline abortion) is 19 per 100,000. The 1973 maternal death rate for hysterotomy abortion is 79.9 per 100,000.[30]

mother, found that the pills she had taken could produce a defective child. Mrs. Sheri Finkbine was scheduled for an abortion at a hospital in Phoenix. After a newspaper reporter had heard her story and the impending tragedy was reported throughout the United States, the Phoenix Hospital cancelled Mrs. Finkbine's abortion. In those days, it was not legal anywhere in these United States (including the states where abortion laws are most liberal) for a woman to have an abortion because a child might be defective. Mrs. Finkbine had an abortion in Sweden where, at that time, it was also illegal on the grounds of an expected defective child.

A number of forces were at work throughout the world but especially in the United States in the decade beginning in 1968. As Stanton puts it:[31] "In the confluence of 'women's liberation,' sexual freedom, and concern for ecology, population and pollution, vast forces inimical to the wellbeing of human embryo and fetus were in motion. The American Law Institute was proffering a little 'reasonable' liberation of the abortion laws to take care of the 'hard' cases, physical and mental health, incest, rape, and genetic defect. The quality of human life ethic gained respectability at the expense of human life itself in socially and academically impeccable circles. As medical indications for abortion evaporated, doctors increasingly invoked mental health as justification for abortion. Undocumented statements, subsequently acknowledged as unfounded in fact, were endlessly repeated until they acquired the ring of truth. Sincere and concerned people were disturbed; they were purposely and purposefully misled. Thousands of women were said to be dying each year at the hands of criminal abortionists. Some estimated 10,000 women died each year of illegal abortion—others said 5,000. The United States Public Health Service, however, reported from *all abortions legal and illegal,* 189 deaths in 1966, 160 deaths in 1967. Obviously inflation had hit the abortion statistics before it hit the grocer's shelf.''

In 1965 the American College of Obstetricians and Gynecologists changed the definition of human pregnancy. Conception ceased to mean fertilization; conception thereafter meant implantation. The terms ''post-conceptive contraception'' (double talk of the highest magnitude) and ''post-conceptive fertility control'' came into being as synonymous with abortion.[32]

One hundred professors of obstetrics in American Medical Schools, in 1972, issued a statement organized by the foundation-funded association for the study of abortion as follows: ''It would be necessary for physicians to realize that abortion has become a predominantly social as well as medical responsibility. For the first time, except for cosmetic surgery, doctors will be expected to do an operation simply because the patient asks that it be done. Granted, this changes the physician's traditional role, but it will be necessary to make this change if we are to serve the new society in which we live.''[33]

One wonders if the signatories of this statement realize that the physicians in Germany who had been willing to carry out what the world eventually called atrocities under the Nazi regime claimed as their eventual defense that they had been acting in conformity with the state's wishes.

THE SUPREME COURT

What is the current legal situation in reference to abortion? The Supreme Court has been making decisions in recent years and months which must be of vital concern to every person. First there was the ruling against prayer in public schools.[34] Now if you are for strong separation of church and state, that might have been to your liking, yet a spinoff from that decision virtually eliminates Bible reading in schools, even as literature, and a generation will now grow up in this country knowing more about the writings of Hemingway and Sartre than of St. Paul. College professors of my acquaintance are appalled that students well qualified for admission to college are unable to identify major characters or books of the Bible. Then the Supreme Court dealt with pornography; or perhaps it would be better to say that they failed to deal with pornography.[35] They sounded such an uncertain note that pornography is still undefined in this country, court cases pile up, but what you and I call pornography still flourishes throughout the land. Next, the Supreme Court ruled that capital punishment was an extraordinary and cruel punishment.[36] It is not my purpose to debate capital punishment here, but it does seem to me that the Supreme Court was overly concerned about the humane treatment for the three murderers killed in the previous six years and had little thought for the effect upon society made by the 78,000 murders that took place in that same period of time. It is interesting that such a high regard for the life of murderers preceded the abortion decision.

These three actions of the Supreme Court differ remarkably from each other. The prayer decision is in conformity with the post-Christian era, but it sets the stage for the erosion of other things that are dear to you and me. Pornography, in the Judeo-Christian perspective, is lawful but not expedient. Capital punishment is thought by many to be a divine precept from the covenant given to Noah in the Old Testament, as I have already said, but whether this is your interpretation or not, the abrogation of capital punishment by the Supreme Court may very well endanger your life.

It is not my primary intention to undermine your faith in the Supreme Court, but I would like to examine with you this area where the laws of man and the laws of God are not synonymous and to sharpen your thinking to be critical of civil authority and eventually to show you some of the

natural consequences which I believe have affected and will
affect your lives in days to come as the morality of this
nation is constantly eroded.

In 1959 in a declaration of human rights, the United Nations passed the following resolution: "The child, by reason
of its physical and mental immaturity, needs special safeguards and care, including appropriate legal protection before as well as after birth."[37] That was the United Nations
in 1959. In 1973, on January 22nd, the Supreme Court of the
United States Roe v. Wade and Doe v. Bolton) announced
essentially that a new personal liberty existed in the
Constitution—the liberty of a woman to procure the termination of her pregnancy at any time in its course on demand.[38] It is interesting that the Supreme Court was not
sure in its decision where the Constitution had provided this
right for a woman but the Supreme Court was very clear
that the Constitution did not mention it explicitly. In spite of
the fact that the Court was extremely vague as to this provision in the Constitution, the Court was not the least bit
unsure that it had the power to proclaim a specific constitutional mandate. It propounded a new doctrine on human
life. It rendered invalid the regulation of abortion in every
state of the union. Some of this legislation went back to the
mid-19th century. Other legislation which was overthrown
was recent and was an indication of the concern of lawmak-
ers in this country concerning the need for protection of the
fetus. Some of the legislation previously valid had been confirmed by popular referenda as for example in the states of
Michigan and North Dakota.

The Supreme Court rulings went far beyond the most
optimistic hopes of the pro-abortionists. In 1963 Glanville
Williams, one of the earliest activists in reference to
abortion-on-demand, proposed to the Abortion Law Reform
Association that abortion be a matter between woman and
physician up to the end of the third month. His proposal was

voted down by the then most radical advocates of abortion. Yet in fewer than ten years the Supreme Court has written into our Constitution a far more radical doctrine.

Here are some of the specifics of the Supreme Court's ruling:

1. Until a developing baby is "viable" or "capable of meaningful life" (whatever that means), a state has no "compelling interest" which justifies it in restricting abortion in any way in favor of the fetus. For six or seven months (not clearly defined) the fetus is denied the protection of law explicit in either the 9th or the 14th Amendments.

2. Even after viability (still not clear) has been reached, the developing baby is not a person "in the whole sense" so even after viability the growing baby is not protected by the guarantee that you and I have in the 14th Amendment that life shall not be taken without due process of law.

3. In spite of the fact that the Court recognized that even a developing baby is not a person in "the whole sense" but nevertheless legally recognizable as having "potential life," a state may not protect a viable human being by preventing an abortion undertaken to preserve the health of the mother. By this statement, a fetus as old as nine months, that is just before delivery, is placed in a position, by this decision, of having his right to life subordinated to the demand for abortion predicated on health. Let me digress here and say that up until the Supreme Court's decision in January of 1973, the definition of health had already reached ludicrous proportions. The slightest upset in the emotional state of a woman contemplating the continuation of a pregnancy was ruled by medical doctors to be an impairment to health.

4. The state may require that all abortions be done by licensed physicians, that after the first trimester of pregnancy they be performed in "licensed facilities," and that after viability (still not defined) of the fetus abortions

may be regulated so long as "health" abortions are not denied. The state was forbidden the previous customary safeguard of requiring review of the abortion decision by a hospital committee or alternatively the concurrence in the decision by two physicians other than the expectant mother's attending physician. In the lesser known decision of the Court, the decision also prohibits the state from requiring that the abortion be done in a hospital licensed by the Joint Committee on Accreditation of Hospitals or indeed that it be in a hospital at all. In other words, a free-standing abortion clinic, without any of the safeguards that medicine has built into policing itself, was permitted.

Justice Blackmun, who wrote the majority opinion, made it abundantly clear that if any religion was to be a guide to him it would be paganism. He alluded to the practice of the Persians, the Greeks, and of the Romans, but he ignored Christianity. The Hippocratic oath which has been taken by physicians for the past 2,000 years specifically prohibits abortion and the suggestion of it. Justice Blackmun laid this aside as having no relevance today.

In reviewing ancient and early Christian views on abortion, Harold O. J. Brown has said:[39] "If it were true that pre-Christian, non-Jewish antiquity did altogether accept abortion in principle and in practice, that would not be a strong argument in favor of our doing likewise; the ancient world accepted quite a number of things that we rightly reject, e.g., the absolute right of the father to decide upon the death of his children, the practice of slavery, torture, and mutilation and the custom of gladiatorial combat." Brown goes on to point out how surprising it was that the court explicitly cited ancient precedents to justify its decision "in the face of the almost universal condemnation of that decision by later, i.e., Hippocratic, Jewish, and Christian, thought."

Perhaps one of the frightening things is that when the Supreme Court relies on the moral views of paganism they are opening the door to infanticide, because those systems and philosophies which permitted abortion also permitted infanticide. Brown also points out that the ancient pagan world was not without some legislation against abortion; indeed, at least two pagan emperors punished abortion with banishment.

The decision takes some comfort in its wording in the fact that the mortality of abortion is even lower than the mortality for live births. The reference, of course, can only apply to the mother; the baby's mortality is 100 percent. (History may prove these statements to be incorrect in reference to maternal mortality.)

Here are some of the direct quotations from the majority opinion of the highest court in our land: "If the state is interested in protection of fetal life after viability it may go so far as to proscribe abortion."[40] It is incredible that the Court would have such a low regard for life, state its callousness so crudely, and do so while exceeding its own constitutional obligation, if not authority.

It is, further, absolutely astounding to me that Justice Blackmun could have included the following sentence in his decision. "We need not resolve the question of when life begins." Indeed need we not! Where does this lead? It leads to infanticide and eventually to euthanasia. If the law will not protect the life of a normal unborn child, what chance does a newborn infant have after birth, if in the eyes of a Justice Blackmun, he might be less than normal? Obviously because the Supreme Court acted in such a way as to ignore the rights of the unborn child, this lack of right continues when the unborn child has been *delivered* by the procedure known as hysterotomy.

When Mr. Blackmun said that the Court was not in a position to speculate on when life begins, he did us a great disservice. The Court really did decide when life begins in that it decided that life does not begin before live birth.

Justice Blackmun also exhibited a rather jaundiced view of motherhood and misplaced his compassion in the following manner: "Maternity, or additional offspring, may force upon the woman a distressful life in the future. Psychological harm may be imminent. Mental and physical health may be taxed by child care. There is also the distress, for all concerned, associated with the unwanted child, and there is the problem of bringing the child into a family already unable, psychologically and otherwise, to care for it." Dean O'Meara of the Notre Dame Law School beautifully disposed of this misplaced emphasis: "Mr. Justice Blackmun seems unconscious of the fact that most women *want* children; the few who don't, and those who don't want any more, need not become pregnant. In view of easily available contraceptive devices, there is only a minimal possibility of unwanted pregnancy. It is incredible that not a single member of the Court mentioned this everyday fact of life. On the contrary, the majority decided on an either/or basis, either the misery of motherhood or abortion. Nonsense."[41]

Dean O'Meara also recognized the myth of privacy and understands full well the semantic brainwashing to which we have been subjected: "No, there is nothing private about an abortion. Yet privacy is what makes an abortion legal. What an upside-down use of the English language!... The Supreme Court simply legislated the legality of abortion and, in seeking a basis for this usurpation of legislative power, seized upon the right of privacy—the reason put forward by the small minority clamoring for what the Court has given them, namely abortion on demand."[42]

The Chief Justice of the Supreme Court, Justice Burger, said, "The vast majority of physicians ... act only on the basis of carefully deliberated medical judgments relating to life and health..."[43] The simple fact of the matter is that the

Chief Justice does not know physicians as well as I do, nor does he appreciate how few physicians it takes to make abortion-on-request equivalent to abortion-on-demand.

Finally, in referring to the woman's right of privacy, Justice Blackmun wrote: "This right of privacy ... is broad enough to encompass a woman's decision whether or not to terminate her pregnancy."[44]

Where does this leave us practically at the moment? At this moment unborn infants have no protection at all anywhere in these United States. There is not the slightest doubt that in the first six to seven months of fetal existence, abortion-on-demand is a constitutional right of a woman. There is not the slightest doubt that the value of an embryo or a fetus is absolutely nothing. Abortion-on-demand after the first six or seven months of fetal existence has been affected by the Court because it has denied personhood to the viable fetus on the one hand and through its broad definition of health on the other. If the seven-month-old fetus is not a person (and the Supreme Court has said it cannot be a person as long as it is a fetus), the physician has only one patient, namely the mother. This is in contradistinction to medical understanding throughout the ages. Now when the physician considers the mother's health, he has to do so in reference to the definition of health given by the World Health Organization:* "a state of complete physical, mental, and social well-being, not simply the absence of illness and disease."[45] Obviously, this gives any physician complete license to perform an abortion with complete protection under the law because he could always hide under the umbrella of the World Health Organization's definition of health in that he was working for the well-being of the

---

*The World Medical Association Oath, popularly called the Declaration of Geneva, states: "I will maintain the utmost respect for human life from the time of its conception."[46] The declaration of Geneva was a response to the Nuremberg trials.

mother. In short, unwantedness can be a death sentence for the baby.

One wonders why the Supreme Court chose *Roe* v. *Wade* for a decision. In a discussion entitled "Abortion: Rights or Technicalities?" Brown had this to say. "The (Supreme) Court was under no strong compulsion to intervene in this process of legislative decision, nor if it did, to make a sweeping decision that would by-pass completely the normal legislative process. It is vain to speculate on why this case was chosen for a Supreme Court decision, but it is interesting to note that at the time it was chosen, the abortion issue was under active consideration across the country, and that the Court's decision was to effect at one stroke the radical change which pro-abortionists were finding it difficult (if not impossible) to achieve in state legislatures or popular referenda. The decision also left opponents of abortion with no apparent alternative other than a constitutional amendment with which to combat it."[47]

The dissenting judges in the Supreme Court decision were eloquent. Justice Byron White summed it up as "raw judicial power."[48] Chief Justice Burger, concurring with the majority, said: "I do not read the Court's holding today as having the sweeping consequences attributed to it by the dissenting justices ... the Court today rejects any claim that the Constitution requires abortion on demand."[49] Obviously, it is clear already that the sweeping consequences have taken place and that the Chief Justice was wrong.

I believe that most people have not thought much about their attitude toward abortion; even those who are vigorously opposed to it sometimes do not have good reasons. Two years ago I had the privilege of preaching at two Roman Catholic masses at Villanova University. It was a tremendous opportunity to speak to about 1,300 young people. I said to them essentially what I am writing here. Afterwards, hundreds of those boys and girls came to me and said exactly the same thing: "I have always been against abortion, but now I know why."

Mr. St. John-Stevas has pointed out how little people really understand what they believe.[50] In speaking of abortion he said, "In the world of people who want to improve matters there is a callousness about this subject which really is horrifying. It's as though they (the liberals) got a blind spot about this unfortunate fetus. But what it really is, is another form of discrimination, and people who would never dream of discriminating on the grounds of color discriminate against the fetus on grounds of size, because what is the fetus but something very small that cannot in fact make its voice heard; therefore, it's brushed aside as being of no importance."

SEMANTICS AND BRAINWASHING

I have already told you some of the medical things you should know about the development of a fetus and the way in which it is killed by abortion. The next thing I think you should know medically is that the idea that abortion is not killing is a new idea. Five years ago, everybody agreed that abortion was killing an unborn baby. Now we have been brainwashed (and I will have more to say about this brainwashing later) so that words do not mean the same things that they used to mean. For example, you find that the abortionists do not talk about babies in the womb except when they have a slip of the tongue. They prefer to call these "fetuses" but even better, when they call the developing baby "the product of conception" it ceases to have a personality and its destruction could not possibly mean killing. As recently as 1967, at the first international conference on abortion, a purely secular group of people said, "We can find no point in time between the union of sperm and egg and the birth of an infant at which point we can say that this is not a human life.''[51] Now if that had been a theological group it would have been easy to understand the statement. But when one considers that this was a secular group of people, representing thoughts from many cultures all over the world, that doctrine is worth listening to.

I should try to follow the advice of M. J. Sobran[52] and use the language that has been understood since the beginning of time. When I say a woman is pregnant, I should refer to that as a woman "with child" because that is indeed what she is. When a woman wants an abortion it is because she does not want a baby. If a woman is pregnant and is asked why she wants an abortion, she says, "Because I don't want a baby." If that "thing" that is within her is not a baby, then what is it? When my scientific colleagues might refer to the product of conception, or embryo, or fetus, I should call it a developing baby or the unborn baby because that is what it is. When my colleagues might refer to the termination of the unborn baby, I should call that what it is, namely killing.

In the world of semantics there has been another peculiar change. When I was just a few years younger, abortion was a terrible word but the term "abortionist" conjured up in one's mind the dregs of humanity with a simple skill that destroyed an unborn baby and degraded society by his very existence. The manner in which the abortionist has been elevated from that picture to being the benefactor of society and the darling of intellectuals is a complicated process. At least part of it is what has happened to society in the past decade. A hedonistic, sexually permissive society would have to change its views on abortion and abortionists in order to pursue the life of convenience, of pleasure, of per-missiveness, of undisciplined morality in order to do away with one of the sequelae of all of these things, namely the unwanted product of that behavior, the unwanted baby.

As an illustration of how we are brainwashed in our understanding of semantics, the Harvard Medical School's Department of Continuing Education announced a course entitled "Advances in Contraception" (October 3-5, 1975, at the Beth Israel Hospital) and listed the topics to be discussed: "Hormonal Contraception," "Intrauterine Devices" (up until that point both of these subjects might be included under the general term "Advances in Contraception," although intrauterine devices are considered by most people to prevent implantation and therefore abortifacient). The next three subjects in no way could be called contraception, when titled "Termination of Pregnancy," "The Legal Aspects of Contraception," "Abortion, and Sterilization, and Population Dynamics."

In this war of semantics, somehow or other liberal thinking has switched the truth that the unborn child is the victim of the abortion to the fact that the mother not wanting a pregnancy somehow or other is the victim of pregnancy. There is a danger in the semantics about abortion being a private matter between "a woman and her physician" ... in fact, there is an added danger in that situation because the nonmedical person in society can slough off the whole moral and ethical issue because it is a physician's decision, and, if so, presumably not a layman's decision. Another strange turn of semantics is the one-sidedness of the belief that abortion is a "private" matter. If we were to say it is a "religious" matter we would be laughed to scorn. On the other hand is there anything more private than one's religion?

Some editorial comment was very frank on the replacement of an old ethic with a new one as well as the dodging of the true meaning of words while semantic changes were taking place.

An editorial in *California Medicine* in September 1970 described the quality of life ethic that was replacing the older absolute value of life ethic this way: "Since the old ethic has not been fully displaced it has been necessary to separate the idea of abortion from the idea of killing, which continues to be socially abhorrent. The result has been a curious avoidance of the scientific fact, which everyone really knows, that human life begins at conception and is continuous where intra- or extrauterine until death. The very considerable semantic gymnastics which are required to rationalize abortion as anything but taking a human life would be ludicrous if they were not often put forth under socially impeccable auspices. It is suggested that this schizophrenic sort of subterfuge is necessary because while a new ethic is being accepted the old one has not yet been rejected."[53]

EXPERIENCE IN OTHER COUNTRIES (AND HERE)

In countries that have gone the way of abortion-on-demand that we are now embarked upon, there have been developments from which we can learn. Japan is one of these countries. They liberalized abortions just about the way we did, but they did it in 1948. The first year there were 250,000 abortions;[54] in the first eight years they had 5,000,000 abortions. Their experience indicates that as people became used to abortions—as it no longer was a shocking thing to talk about, and as people talked about the products of conception rather than talking about an unborn baby—abortions took place later and later in pregnancy. By 1956, 26,000 abortions in Japan were at five months, 20,000 were at six months, and 7,000 were at seven months.[55] In 1972 there were no fewer than 1,500,000 abortions. Dr. T. A. Ueno, professor at Nihan University in Tokyo, said:

"We can now say that the law is a bad one." He remarked at the International Academy of Legal and Social Medicine at its meeting in Rome: "The sooner Japan returns to a solid law which forbids the taking of the life of the unborn, the better for our nation."[56]

Poland has had a very liberal abortion law for many years, but recently the government reversed itself because they realized they were facing genocide. So many people were having abortions in Poland that the population had fallen well below the "population zero" fertility rate. We have essentially reached that same rate.

In Czechoslovakia only one woman in ten uses any kind of contraceptive measures. Czechoslovakia has had a long history of free abortion and recently has begun to tighten its rather liberal policy. There has been a rising incidence of premature births due to cervical scarring, which is one of the results of repeated abortions. Doctors Vedra and Zidofsky of the Institute for the Care of Mother and Child in Prague, report a rise in premature deliveries. They say repeated abortions can have two effects: the cervix can become damaged and weakened, leading to spontaneous abortion or premature delivery; or the cavity of the uterus can become damaged, leading to the formation of scar tissue and spontaneous abortion. "Another consequence of the abortion situation is that a growing number of children are born prematurely and must attend special schools because they are not as intelligent as their fullterm peers."[57] A later report from Czechoslovakia covering a seventeen-year period says: "Artificial termination of pregnancy greatly increases the risk of a subsequent, spontaneous abortion."[58] This is based on a study of 2,000,000 abortions carried out in the first trimester.

The Supreme Court's decision enabling free-standing abortion clinics to exist has made it very difficult to keep records in the United States on how many abortions are being carried out and what the complications might be. The National Health Service in Great Britain keeps excellent records and they have been in the abortion-on-demand business for about six years. The pro-abortionists in this country, in the days before the Supreme Court's decision, told us of how there would be a reduction in illegitimacy, prostitution, venereal disease, and other social ills. Unfortunately, the excellent records of the first five years of liberalized abortion under the National Health Service in Great Britain have revealed an increase in incidence of the following: illegitimacy, venereal disease, prostitution, later sterility of the previously aborted mother, pelvic inflammatory disease from gonorrhea, and subsequent spontaneous abortions or miscarriages. Ectopic pregnancies—that is, where the egg is fertilized not in the uterus but up in the fallopian tube, requiring an emergency abdominal operation—have doubled since abortion has been liberalized. Prematurity in women who have had a previous abortion has increased in Great Britain by 40 percent.[59] No one has done a study on the emotional reaction or the guilt of the woman who has had an abortion and now desperately wants a baby that she cannot have.

In May 1975, the National Academy of Sciences' Institute of Medicine issued a study in reference to the effect of legalized abortion on the health of the women who were aborted. The study was the subject of a critique by Harold O. J. Brown in *Human Life Review* and he reported that the study was funded by the militantly pro-abortion Population Council and that the council's senior consultant, Dr. Christopher Tietze, was a member of the National Academy's steering committee on legalized abortion. Dr. Brown's concluding paragraph is this: "It is remarkable that a report that ignores major information relatively available in a good medical library in order to give unwarranted reassurances concerning the potential medical and psychological consequences of a widespread procedure (the second most common surgical procedure in America today, following tonsillectomy) should be published under the aegis of the National Academy of Science. This is all the more remarkable in view of the report's repeated admission that it draws upon inadequate evidence. One is led to wonder whether its publication was not rushed in order to make it available in time to influence pending legislation. In light of its apparently tendentious content, it may not be unreasonable to inquire whether the participation of the Population Council in the financing and of Dr. Christopher Tietze on the steering committee may have inclined the present report in the direction of advocacy rather than objectivity. In any case, it is particularly difficult to reconcile the omission of readily available, important material such as that provided by Kotasek and Lembrych* with the standard of scientific inquiry and academic integrity that one would expect from the National Academy of Sciences.''[60]

For completeness of the international view of abortion, a word concerning the action of the German high court is in order.

The Federal Constitutional Court of Western Germany held abortion to be a "homicidal act" and overturned the liberalized abortion law enacted by the German Parliament. In June 1974 the West German Federal Diet (Bundestag) passed "The Fifth Law for the Reform of the Penal Code" which included a substantial revision of the law relating to abortion.

Harold O. J. Brown in comparing the action of the U. S. Supreme Court with that of the West German Federal Constitutional Court in an action the latter took in June 1974 had this to say: "... The West German Federal Constitutional

---

*Czechoslovakian scientists with extraordinarily broad experience with abortion.

Court dealt with the question of unlimited right to abortion on demand on the basis of an evaluation of fundamental questions concerning the nature of man and the requirements of justice, which the courts held to be reflected in the German Federal Constitution. The decision of the American Court represents a deliberate avoidance of the larger moral, ethical, and anthropological questions to which the German Court addressed itself.... The comparison between the American and German Courts' thinking on the issue is especially disappointing. No one familiar with *Roe* v. *Wade* can fail to recognize that in it the highest American court has evaded the basic moral issue and resolved a fundamental question only on the basis of technical legal construction."[61]

ARGUMENTS
AND ANSWERS

The abortion question is argued on at least four grounds: medical, social, personal, and theological.

The three medical questions that are usually asked of someone in my position who is anti-abortion have to do with rape, suicide, and handicapped children. As horrible a bit of violence as rape is, it very seldom results in pregnancy. A study in Minneapolis of 3,500 consecutive rapes revealed not a single pregnancy.[62] The same is true of maternal suicide. A study over seventeen years in Minneapolis revealed that suicides in reference to pregnancy were part of generalized psychoses and in the rare instance where it did occur did so after pregnancy rather than during. In Czechoslovakia, out of 86,000 induced abortions, twenty-two were done for rape.[63] Finally, studies on handicapped children have indicated that their frustrations are no greater than those experienced by perfectly normal children. To this latter fact I can attest. My life has been spent with children who are less than one would consider totally normal and I have considered it a privilege to be involved with extending the life of these youngsters. In the thousands of such circumstances in which I have participated, I have never had a parent ask me why I tried so hard to save the life of their defective child. Now that I am seeing children I operated upon years ago bring me their children for care, I have never had an old patient ask me why I worked so hard to save his or her life. Nor has a parent *ever* expressed to me the wish that his child had not been saved.

The following letter to the editor appeared in the *Daily Telegraph* in London on December 8, 1962, when the Thalidomide tragedy was being discussed in European newspapers and abortion was sought as an easy way to get rid of the possibly defective babies:

> Trowbridge
> Kent
> December 8, 1962

Sirs:

We were disabled from causes other than Thalidomide, the first of us having two useless arms and hands; the second, two useless legs; and the third, the use of neither arms nor legs.

We were fortunate ... in having been allowed to live and we want to say with strong conviction how thankful we are that none took it upon themselves to destroy us as useless cripples.

Here at the Delarue school of spastics, one of the schools of the National Spastic Society, we have found worthwhile and happy lives and we face our future with confidence. Despite our disability, life still has much to offer and we are more than anxious, if only metaphorically, to reach out toward the future.

This, we hope, will give comfort and hope to the parents of the Thalidomide babies, and at the same time serve to condemn those who would contemplate the destruction of even a limbless baby.

> Yours faithfully,
> Elane Duckett
> Glynn Verdon
> Caryl Hodges

It is in the social arena that the abortion question is most ardently debated. Here a small minority of pro-abortionists have altered our vocabulary, misrepresented statistics, reprehensibly made false associations—and with such great success that they influenced the Supreme Court to perpetrate on the American people, who are fundamentally pro-life, the legalized murder of millions of babies in the name of progress and social reform. You will be told that the Gallup poll has found that "two out of three Americans now favor legal abortion."[64] Dr. Gallup compared the results of a poll taken in June 1972 with his previous polls on abortion. However, he was not honest enough to state that he had changed the questions. Dr. Gallup polled Americans on abortion in 1962, 1965, 1968, and 1969.[65] In all of these polls, he asked identical questions. The record shows that in the years 1965, 1968 and 1969, 68 percent to 74 percent of all Americans opposed abortion done solely for the reason of family economic distress. In similar fashion 79 percent to 91 percent of all Americans questioned, disapproved abortion for the reason of pregnancy being unwanted. Then in June 1972, Dr. Gallup changed his question and framed it in terms of abortion being a private matter. He did not ask the same question as in the previous polls but nevertheless proclaims a vast shift in public opinion. I suspect that Dr. Gallup is framing public opinion rather than sampling it.

Time Magazine also reported on the news release that had

appeared in the Washington *Post* in their issue of September 4, 1972. The accuracy of the article was challenged in *Time* on October 19, 1972; the following statement appeared on behalf of the editors: "Be assured our intention in publishing the Gallup findings was not to lead our readers astray. Obviously, *Time* has no say how the Gallup poll words its questionnaires. That the wording was changed this year may well reflect the need to gauge the temper of the times from another angle. In any case, Gallup interpreted the findings to say in a general sense that American attitudes toward birth control are changing; we were reflecting their interpretations in our brief report."[66]

In view of what I have written above concerning *Time* Magazine, it is significant that *Time* did not print a single word about the size of the victory at the polls in Michigan and in North Dakota when abortion was turned down in public referenda. In November of 1972 Michigan citizens voted on a proposal allowing abortion on demand up to twenty weeks (not the much more liberal interpretation of the Supreme Court). This was rejected by a 61 percent vote.* Parenthetically, let me say that just a few weeks before, the polls in that state indicated that abortion legalization would win by 25 points. The vote in the opposite direction was probably tremendously influenced by a state-wide educational program undertaken by a coalition of pro-life forces.

*Facts on the American vote on abortion on request:[67] November 7, 1972

	Pro-Life		Anti-Life	
Massachusetts (17 selected communities)	93,669	44%	118,568	56%
Michigan (statewide)	1,843,363	61%	1,175,830	39%
North Dakota (statewide)	191,792	79%	58,543	21%
Total American vote on Abortion November 7, 1972			3,482,195	100%
Pro-Life Vote			*2,129,254*	*61.1%*
Anti-Life Vote			1,352,941	38.9%

You will be told that doctors favor abortion on demand. As a back-up to this statement you will be told that the AMA approves abortion. Perhaps you do not know that only 42 percent of our nation's 386,000 doctors pay dues to the AMA.

You will be told that abortion reduces maternal deaths and, along the same lines, that unwanted pregnancy produces psychoses in pregnant women. The late Dr. Alan Gutmacher, one of the most ardent pro-abortion physicians in the land, has said the following: "Today it is possible for almost any patient to be brought through pregnancy alive, unless she suffers from a fatal illness such as cancer or leukemia, and if so, abortion would be unlikely to prolong, much less save life."[68] And then in reference to psychosis, Gutmacher said: "There is *little* evidence that pregnancy itself worsens a psychosis, either intensifying it or rendering a prognosis for full recovery less likely."[69] Dr. Gutmacher was president of Planned Parenthood World Population and the one who moved Planned Parenthood into the abortion field.

You will be told that already the liberalized abortion laws have reduced infant deaths. This is like suggesting amputation of the leg in normal men to prevent ankle fractures while skiing. It is not possible to save one child's life by killing another. Obviously if one does 1,000,000 abortions, none of those unknown babies will ever become infant deaths since none of them will ever live to be infants.

You will be introduced to situational ethics from academic sources considered to be above reproach. Dr. Mary Ellen Avery, professor of pediatrics at Harvard University and physician-in-chief of Boston Children's Hospital, writing in the *New England Journal of Medicine,* suggests that if on abortion the infant is large enough to survive with the extraordinary care provided by an intensive care unit, the physician should make the decision about caring for the child or not caring for the child or whether or not the parents wish the child to survive.[70] In other words, wantedness is the test for survival. Incidentally the Boston Children's Hospital is now in the ludicrous situation of having one of the world's most sophisticated intensive care units for premature babies with an enviable record in survival and yet they have opened their doors to teen-age girls demanding abortion in the first trimester. Throughout the land unborn babies are being aborted (killed) at the same moment that others, delivered prematurely, are being given the most sophisticated extraordinary care in an effort to keep them alive. Wantedness is the criterion of choice.

You will be told that a liberalized abortion attitude will encourage the widespread use of contraception until the need for abortion disappears. Such is not the case. In Japan about half the Japanese women who have abortions admit that they did not even try to prevent conception.[71] Dr. Gutmacher said: "Those who favor liberalization want to substitute safe abortions for the dangerous, clandestine variety until contraception is so widely practiced that unwanted pregnancy—and therefore the need for abortion—disappears."[72] Simple logic and very little understanding of human nature should remind everyone that easily available abortion decreases the use of contraceptives rather than increasing their use, and obviously the demand for abortion increases as a result.

Contraception is something that prevents the union of sperm and egg; it is not abortion. Contraception and family planning in the larger sense come under the heading of sexual ethics, while abortion has to do with human rights. If this is true, and I believe most firmly that it is, what one does in the matter of birth control or contraception is up to the individual to decide on the basis of his own conscience.

However, once conception has taken place, then the consideration of abortion moves out of the field of sexual ethics and directly into the field of human rights.

In all of these social discourses you will be introduced to the war of semantics. In 1974, in December, Donald P. Warwich, chairman of the Department of Sociology and Anthropology of York University, Toronto, wrote on the "Moral Message of Bucharest," which was a report on the International Congress on Population.[73] He called attention to the fact that "population studies" is a euphemism of family planning research; "family planning," a cover for birth control; abortion (itself a euphemism of feticide) is called a "retrospective method of fertility limitation."

Reporting further on the conference, he said: "Donors claim to be supporting programs aimed at helping couples to obtain their own reproductive goals, when, in fact, most of the money goes for limiting births. Social scientists carry out methodically dubious knowledge-attitude-practice surveys with the frank intention of generating data to show the need for family planning programs and draw totally unwarranted conclusions from their findings. Private organizations subvert their own proprieties and compromise their independence to take advantage of easy population money. Researchers give evidence of suppressing findings which deviate from donor expectations or which would embarrass the host country."[74] It is much easier to think of killing "the product of conception" rather than destroying an embryo. It would also be easier to kill a fetus than to kill an unborn baby. Beware that you do not fall into the trap of thinking of abortion as a legitimate method of birth control and of population control.

There are countless other social misrepresentations that you may be presented with but the ultimate one will have to do with overpopulation. Overpopulation is certainly a major concern but it is not overpopulation that is our problem; it is the distribution of the world's population. I would suggest that when someone talks to you about this subject you ask: "What country are you most concerned about?" He will practically always answer: "India." Then you can introduce an interesting statistic. New Jersey is twice as crowded as India and it will take two hundred years of population growth which the United States was experiencing five years ago before these United States will be as uncomfortably crowded as New Jersey.

I began this book by suggesting that our society might be schizophrenic. As further indication that this is not far from the case, remember that the Supreme Court has declared the unborn baby to be a nonperson. Yet, a paternity action can be brought by a pregnant woman as soon as she knows she is pregnant. Some states have statutes on their books that say that the abortionist must make every effort to resuscitate the baby he has just aborted. An unborn baby can be injured in an accident and at a later date, after he is born, can sue the person who injured him. A fetus can inherit an estate and take precedence over a person who is already born, as soon as that fetus is himself born.

How is it that if a man gets a woman pregnant and she wants the baby, he can be sued for support? Why can't he say, "I don't think I'm mature enough to be a father"? Why can't he say, "It's part of her body, not mine"? If he just walks out of the responsibility of being a father, at least no one's life is terminated. On the other hand, if the woman in question says she is not ready to be a mother, all she has to do is go to an abortionist and the whole thing is over, including life for the baby.

You will be told that you are emotionalizing the issue. M. J. Sobran concludes an article in the *Human Life Review* with a statement about this which must be quoted in its entirety for full effect: "How to handle the charge that we are 'emotionalizing the issue.' Like this, I think: 'In a sense, that is true. I don't want to make the issue so emotional that we can't think clearly, but I confess that I want to bring the discussion down to earth, where people often do get emotional when they realize what is being talked about. I think, for instance, that there are circumstances when a woman may rightfully kill her own unborn child, just as there are instances when a man might be justified in killing his aged father. But we ought never to lose sight of the essential horror of such acts even when they are called for. And I think your abstract vocabulary makes us lose sight of that horror. What is more, I think your vocabularly is *intended* to make us lose sight of it. Big words do tend to numb us, as George Orwell has complained, and we can then quote as much as we like of "politics and the English language," by which time the humane and generous sentiments of our audience will have recognized the pro-abortionist for the moral idiot he is. As Mark Twain wrote, "I know that I am prejudiced in this matter, but I would be ashamed of myself if I were not." There are matters on which neutrality is unthinkable. The sanctity of life is one. The "prejudice" in favor of life is so deep, so much in our speech, in our bones, that its suspension is an unnatural act. The burden of proof must be put on the neutralizers, and it can be done without any strain on our part. Our audience—the American public—is on our side, often without knowing it.' "[75]

In any discussion in a social realm concerning abortion you will be exposed to some smoke screens; things that people set up so that they can talk about abortion. One of these will be a discussion of meaningful life. Who can say whose life is meaningful? You must be careful that some critic does not come along and consider our lives to be "without meaning." Think of people such as Franklin Roosevelt, Napoleon, Hellen Keller, or perhaps someone in your own family who was thought at one time not to have a meaningful life, yet, with the passage of time, made fantastic contributions to history. You will be told that restrictive abortion laws work to the detriment of the poor. Yet, in the first year that abortion was liberalized in New York City, the majority of women who were aborted were middle class, white, single, widowed, or divorced women who wanted their abortions for reasons of convenience that were non-medical.[76] The women's liberation movement is frequently wrapped up around the abortion issue and whether you are for or against women's lib, do not get the baby and the bath water mixed up. Eventually the old argument that restrictive laws are merely made to be broken and therefore should be removed will be brought to your attention. There are two answers to that. The first is that we have laws against murder which people break but that does not mean that the laws against murder should be removed. Secondly, if a legal abortion cannot be obtained and it is assumed that a criminal abortion will be substituted for it, the answer is that you do not fight the crime of legal abortion with the immorality of abortion-on-demand.

You will recall that the Supreme Court invoked the "right of privacy" as the telling argument in making its decision. Along these lines, first among the personal arguments frequently reiterated is the woman's declaration, "I want the right to my own body." Apart from the obvious suggestion that the right to her body begins considerably before the need for an abortion there are other concerns. Ultimate sexual freedom leads to the demand for abortion but without consideration of the rights of the product of that freedom, namely, the unborn baby. The fact of the matter is that the child in the womb is not a part of the woman's body, subject to her absolute control. She provides the environment and the sustenance but this sustenance does not go to a subhuman creature devoid of human rights.

It is interesting that women claim that they are personally exploited when a man gets them pregnant. Yet these same women do not realize that abortion exploits them still more. Abortion provides a new business in another kind of feminine prostitution. So says Mary R. Joyce who claims that the sexual revolution is yet to begin. She claims that when women prostitute themselves to what is called the "baby scrambler," the suction machine for abortion, they give their money to men more often than not. She further quotes that in New York City alone, doctors in hospitals made approximately $140,000,000 in the first year-and-a-half of New York's liberalized abortion laws. Mrs. Joyce is convinced that if women were not so intellectually passive, they would be able to see through their new so-called liberation very clearly.[77]

I have already spoken of the simple theology which leads me to my position. I am distressed that some of the major denominations in the Protestant faith in our country have been brainwashed along with the rest of our population concerning abortion. The right of privacy has been stressed by the Supreme Court. A United Presbyterian committee said, "Abortion of a nonviable fetus is not a legal matter. A woman, her doctor, her minister or counselor should decide." Now, that is so private that they left the father out of consideration. The Methodists said: "Abortion and sterilization are the decisions of those most concerned." But the Methodists forget the baby.

ABORTION IS NOT A ROMAN CATHOLIC ISSUE

When I speak to almost any audience about abortion I start off by acknowledging the fact that I am not a Roman Catholic. Now why should I do this? It is because abortion has been forced by the press, pro-abortionists, and those concerned about church-state relations into a Roman Catholic mold so that the uncommitted on this issue "understand" that abortion is a Roman Catholic issue. Because the Roman Catholic Church opposes abortion, abortion has become a Catholic issue, in spite of the fact that many Jews and many Protestants feel equal revulsion on the matter of abortion. Indeed there has been almost a backlash on the anti-abortion movement by liberals profiting from the bigotry of non-Catholics when they are in essence asked would you rather be Catholic or right?

It is important to recognize that anti-abortion movements featuring Roman Catholic participants are at grass root levels; although the Roman Catholic hierarchy may be against abortion it is not directing its constituency into opposition in a public protesting forum.

M. J. Sobran[78] has called attention to the fact that the New York *Times* carried a story about a father and son named Spear who refused to accept advertising from, or give news coverage to, any political candidate who favored permissive abortion. The Spears ran a small newspaper in upper New York State. Father and son gave as their reason "people are killing people." The New York *Times* quoted the Spears and then said, "The Spears are Roman Catholics." Obviously the implication is that the Spears feel the way they do only because they are Roman Catholics and, therefore, their opinion on this matter is open to some suspicion. It is another example of how the press does not take a neutral position on the matter of abortion.

Being against abortion has somehow or other become being against the poor, against women, for the Catholic Church, or being bigoted on a very private matter. M. J. Sobran has covered this so well that he must be quoted. After a clear presentation of the aforementioned statement in the New York *Times* and then fanciful presentation of not-so-absurd absurdities Mr. Sobran concluded:

"Catholics do tend to favor the prohibition of abortion, Negroes to desire Civil Rights legislation, Jews to call for guarantees for the safety of Israel. Yet to ascribe to any man a state of intellectual servility that reduces his opinion to an index of his social place and affiliation, is, quite simply, a breach of good manners and good taste. It is to suggest that no man can have an honest and intelligent opinion on any issue that touches him closely." In a few words Sobran understands full well the war of semantics in which we are engaged: "One of the most dangerous mistakes the enemy of abortion can make is to adopt the phraseology of the pro-abortionist. 'Fetus' and 'abortion' are obvious examples. They should be used only among those who agree on their moral meaning; otherwise, they work in favor of him who would deny the humanity of the unborn child, simply by putting the burden of proof on him who asserts that humanity. Such neutral words are convenient for promoting that psychological ooze in which it is possible for judgment to be suspended: suspended not provisionally but *in principle....* When we talk about 'aborting fetuses' instead of 'killing children' we have given (the skeptic) a good edge, simply by emptying our language of substance.... We can win the abortion argument simply by speaking the plain English of custom and of our countrymen, and by avoiding the assumption that we must somehow justify ourselves in the gilded pseudolanguage of the doctrinaire. *Call* the unborn child a child, and *dare* the abortionist to deny it. He will find that if he does, he ruptures that inarticulate consensus that underlies and animates the speech of ordinary people, the piety and realism that recognized the magical kinship between the man in the street and the man in the womb. Then it will be he, and not we, enemies of prenatal murder, who will be up against all the might of poetry, opposing the cant of progress, individual choice, and a woman's right over her own body to the supreme power in human affairs."[79]

ABORTION
AND THE PRESS

The press just does not carry reports which are anti-abortion. Examples are given in this text in reference to the lack of reaction of *Time* Magazine to the significance of the referenda on abortion in Michigan and North Dakota which turned out to be overwhelmingly pro-life. Another example is the fact that the New York *Times* did not carry a single word about an internationally significant bit of news in the effort of Senator Helms to prevent the use of tax money for abortion programs overseas.[80] His amendment said in part: (Sec. 116) "... None of the funds made available to carry out this part will be used in any manner, directly or indirectly, to pay for abortions, abortifacient drugs or devices, the promotion of the practice of abortion, or the supportive research designed to develop methods of abortion. Provisions of this section shall not apply to any funds allocated prior to the date of its enactment."[81]

The newsletter of Americans United for Life reported a segment of Senator Helms' speech in support of his amendment which was adopted unanimously by voice vote. The fact that it was adopted unanimously by voice vote is another example of the schizophrenia which reigns in our government in view of the Supreme Court's decision on abortion. Here is Senator Helms' comment: "Mr. President, the amendment which I propose is very simple and straightforward. It is intended to prevent the use of A.I.D. (Agency for International Development) funds—that is to say, funds collected from the taxpayers of the United States—in the practice and promotion of abortion.

"At the present time, A.I.D. supports abortion in at least three major ways. First, A.I.D. supports, in many individual countries, population programs of which abortion is one of the approved methods of population control. Second,

A.I.D. is a major supporter of international organizations and funding mechanisms which provide training programs, hospital facilities and equipment for performing abortions, and propaganda programs to make abortions culturally acceptable in foreign countries. Third, A.I.D. funds research both in the United States and abroad aimed at developing cheap methods of abortion, principally through so-called abortifacient drugs, that is, chemicals which induce abortion. The research in this third category is envisioned by A.I.D. as developing a pill or simple self-administered drug which should become the primary method of population control throughout the world. Unlike the pill which is merely contraceptive, this will be the pill that kills.

"My amendment would therefore stop the use of U. S. Government funds to promote and develop ways of killing unborn children."[82]

Obviously this is significant news that should have been picked up by the media.

A newsletter of the Americans United for Life also carries an excerpt from a letter of October 25, 1973, by Senator Helms to Daniel K. Parker, administrator of the Agency for International Development: "The A.I.D. paper states that my amendment would represent a fundamental change in U.S. policy regarding population assistance. On the contrary, Congress has never authorized the killing of unborn children as a means of population control. I doubt that anyone ever thought that the Foreign Assistance Act would be used to promote abortion when it was passed. As far as domestic policy is concerned, Congress has specifically forbidden the use of abortion and family planning research."[83]

In the New York *Times,* April 12, 1975, Professor Cyril Means, writing of abortion, attacks people whom he calls "fetophiles." He goes on and speaks of "those within the Roman Catholic Church and their fellow travelers on this issue." This absurd statement would indicate that an Orthodox Jew or a conservative Protestant are classed as "fellow travelers" with Roman Catholics by Professor Means.

When Dr. Kenneth Edelin was found guilty of manslaughter by a jury in Boston, Massachusetts, after he had allegedly permitted a baby to die in the process of being aborted by the hysterotomy technique, the newspapers raised a hue and cry on the basis of religious, racial and social bias, in Boston, on the part of the jury, etc.

NATURAL CONSEQUENCES

I have talked of the law and I have certainly talked of life. Now, I would like to say a few things about the days ahead. There are a number of things that have happened and will continue to happen because of the action of the Supreme Court in favor of abortion on demand.

First of all the law will look ridiculous. Several weeks after the decision, a young woman boarded an airplane in Pittsburgh and flew to Youngstown, Ohio, a flight of thirty-two minutes. During that time she delivered a baby and left it in the restroom of the airplane. Now, if she had had an abortion in Pittsburgh, before she got on the plane, she would have been the darling of Planned Parenthood. But thirty-two minutes later, with a natural birth of a premature baby in the state of Ohio, she was sought on two charges, child abandonment and attempted murder. Since then it has been ruled that a minor female may have an abortion on demand without the consent of her parents, yet the law also demands that her parents are responsible for the bill. And even more ridiculous from the point of view of the law is the fact that the unborn baby, being a nonperson, is nevertheless eligible at his mother's request for welfare. To further illustrate the schizophrenic state of the law, the Boston *Globe,* March 20, 1975, contained an advertisement for ear piercing for earrings with this statement, "All we ask is that you sign a special consent form. If you are 18 or younger, you must have your parent's written consent."[85]

Living reported that a Superior Court jury unanimously awarded a three-year-old girl $31,200 in support damages from a doctor who failed in 1971 to correctly perform an abortion that would have prevented her birth.[84] The jury also awarded the mother $10,000 in general damages. Actual damages found by the jury totaled $82,400 but the total was cut in half by the jury when it was found out that the mother was 50 percent responsible for the failure of the abortion. It is difficult to understand by what conceivable right an unborn child who had no say in the fact that she wanted to live or die, when surviving an attempted murder, may sue the attempted killer for not being a more efficient killer.

Second, liberty leads to license. Within a week of the decision of the Supreme Court, the New York Medical Society took a stand in reference to the patient's right to die, but at the discretion of the patient's family—not at the discretion of the patient. Now, you can imagine what that can lead to.[86]

Third, the right to die leads to the right to kill in mercy. In March of 1973, two months after the Supreme Court decision, a Dutch jury found a physician guilty of killing her mother when she had terminal cancer. The victim of the mercy killing was not in pain, but she was just tired of it all. The sentence was a one-week suspended sentence in prison.[87]

A fourth effect of the action of the Supreme Court in reference to abortion is that it will contribute first to the process of depersonalization and secondly to the process of dehumanization. There are a number of episodes in the history of man of which we are all ashamed. Indeed, if we had the chance to act otherwise, we would do so if given that opportunity. Yet, at the time, not only were these things legal, but they were accepted by the people and were even proved to be logical to those few who complained. Jews were considered to be nonpersons in Nazi Germany. Indians were not thought to be persons in the United States. The same Supreme Court to which I have referred so frequently, in the Dred Scott decision in 1857, declared the Negro to be a piece of chattel property.[88] They would have been more honest if they had said nonpeople. Lt. Calley, when accused of unwarranted killing of Vietnamese civilians, expressed the opinion that the Vietnamese were not human beings.[89] Now the Supreme Court tells us that unborn babies are not persons in our society. So we regard the unborn baby today in the way we once looked at the Indian and the Negro and in the same way that the Nazis saw the Jews. In all of these areas, if persons had treated other persons *as* persons and if they had stood for the preservation of life, there would have been no slavery, no Dred Scott decision, no Wounded Knee, and no Nazi Germany guilty of atrocities against Jews.

Fifth, there will be enormous numbers of abortions. Because we do not keep accurate records, I cannot give you the exact number of abortions that have taken place in this country since January 1973, but using the statistics of the abortionists, it is over 3,000,000.*

Sixth, there has been and there will continue to be a change in sexual attitudes. You cannot have over a million abortions taking place every year without everybody knowing about the process. It seems to me inevitable that the social attitudes of our young people will change. There will always be a way out if contraception does not work or if it is not used. Already here in our community, the advertising media make pregnancy a loathsome thing. As you leave the

---

*Statistics on abortion: 1620 abortions per 1000 live births in Washington, D.C., 1679 abortions per 1000 live births in New York State.[90]

airport in Philadelphia and drive into the center of town, you see on billboards and on the tops of taxicabs, the following sign: "Pregnant? For abortion information, call number - - -." The week after the Supreme Court decision, there appeared this headline in the Philadelphia *Bulletin:*[91] "Abortion Study to Be Included in the New Girl Scout Program." The article went on to say the Girl Scouts were planning a new merit badge, a section of which recommends that the older scouts visit an abortion clinic and familiarize themselves with birth control. The President of the Girl Scouts of Philadelphia said the badge was "relevant and proper education for the youngsters." These were girls in the seventh to tenth grades.

Seventh, I believe the door is open to a number of things that, like abortion, are disturbing to a large segment of our population. You may not be immediately aware of the fact that it has been the custom in this country when some private activity was repugnant to the moral sensitivity of the American people, to pass legislation against it. That is why we have laws against such seemingly private engagements as homosexuality, sodomy, prostitution, and adultery. Did you realize that there are also laws prohibiting activities quite lawful in other countries today and in our country in days gone by? I refer to gambling, the taking of addictive drugs, cockfighting, bullfighting and dueling. There are even laws against suicide! Some of these things are done essentially in private. But they are outlawed because they offend other people who know about them.

Eighth, the newborn infant who is not perfect is probably the next target. Remember the Supreme Court left the distinction between feticide and infanticide very hazy by refusing to come to grips with the time that life begins. In May of 1973, in the Johns Hopkins magazine, right after the Supreme Court decision, the following was set out in a box in large type for emphasis, "If the family and the medical staff

agree not to treat a child, assuming he is going to die any-
way, then why not make sure he dies as quickly and painlessly as possible? I think there is little difference between
euthanasia and passive euthanasia."[92] And later the same
month, *Time* Magazine reported a quotation by a Nobel
Prize winner, James D. Watson, the same man who dis-
covered the double helix DNA in the genetic code. *Time*
quoted Dr. Watson's statement that appeared in *Prism*
magazine, which is a publication of the American Medical
Association: "If a child were not declared alive until three
days after birth, then all parents could be allowed the choice
only a few are given under the present system. The doctor
could allow the child to die if the parents so choose and save
a lot of misery and suffering. I believe this view is the only
rational, compassionate attitude to have."[93]

Ninth, abortion is back in the hands of the abortionists.
As I indicated previously, the pro-abortionists use as one of
their chief arguments, the terrible plight of those who had
abortions at the hands of illegal abortionists in their offices,
back rooms, etc. Now the less publicized decision of the
two that the Supreme Court made (*Doe* v. *Bolton*) threw out
the safeguards of having abortions in a hospital that is
accredited and in the mainstream of medical practice. Freedom to establish independent abortion clinics now exists.
Philadelphia was rocked with scandals ranging from kick-
backs for referral to the willingness of a free-standing abortion clinic to do an abortion on a reporter from the *Evening
Bulletin* who was not even pregnant. It is again inevitable
that abortions will largely be done legally by those who
recently did them illegally. I recently saw a title in one of the
opinion magazines entitled, "Suddenly, I'm a legal abortionist."

In a TV program hosted by William F. Buckley, called
"Firing Line," taped in New York City on March 31,
1975,[94] Mr. St. John-Stevas of England answered a question

by Mr. Buckley by stating that two journalists in Great Britain who were not particularly on one side or the other of the abortion issue began an investigation which so horrified them that they turned into "raving anti-abortionists." They published a book called *Babies for Burning*. According to Mr. St. John-Stevas, the journalists reported on a lady who went around to abortionists asking for advice although she had never been pregnant in her life. She was told that all the pregnancy tests she was given were positive, so that she would be able to have an abortion, which of course she did not need. Never at any of these times when she was investigating private abortion clinics was she given any counseling or advice or even any indication that there was an alternative to having an abortion. Mr. St. John-Stevas concluded, "So these really are rackets of the worst possible kind."

Consider for a moment how safe abortion has become for the abortionist. In the days when he was an "illegal abortionist" his motive was profit but with legal punishment hanging over his head, were he caught, he took no chances, humanly speaking, with the expectant mother's life. Now those chances are justified because the law says technically that he has the right to do what the mother says is her right, namely to kill her unborn child.

Tenth, and finally, the phrase of the pro-abortionists that annoys me most is the term "meaningful life." It was said that non-viable babies had no meaningful life. Well, they do. For these small, moving products of abortion that look just as you and I do were used for scientific experiments until recent legislation forbade it.

Paul Ramsey has said: "Here we have an entity, too alive to be dead, not mature enough to be a viable baby, yet human enough to be specially protectible."[95]

Casper W. Weinberger, when Secretary of Health, Education and Welfare, in July of 1975 approved a set of rules

and regulations having to do with certain aspects of research
on human subjects, including fetuses. The report included
the recommendation to the National Commission for the
Protection of Human Subjects of Biomedical and Be-
havioral Research. This commission existed as an expres-
sion of the concern of Congress that "unconscionable acts
involving the fetus may have been performed in the name of
scientific inquiry."[96] This same report in the Federal Register described a study done in Finland, presumably financed
through funds made available by HEW, in which well developed human fetuses were decapitated, after which the
severed heads were attached to a blood oxygenator in order
to keep the head "alive" for the duration of an experiment.
Harold O. J. Brown called attention to the fact that "this
description could be published in the Federal Register without outcry only because we are now thoroughly habituated
to the use of the Latin lone word *fetus* as a kind of *terminus
technicus* free of ethical or emotional connotations. To publish this so naturally would be impossible, of course, if instead of the Latin *fetus* we consistently use its English equivalent, 'young,' or 'offspring'—not to mention 'unborn
child'!"[97]

When facts are really known, action takes place. The
State of California, which has to be considered among the
liberal states in reference to abortion, has banned all experimentation on the living aborted fetus. This bill did not
have a single dissenting vote in either house of the California legislature and was signed into law by the governor.[98]

CHANGING ATTITUDES

The implications go far beyond these ten prophecies
which are already coming true. The trouble begins for you
and me when there is acceptance of the fact that there is

such a thing as life which is not worthy to be lived. The abortion movement in Germany began about 1900 and it had the significant support of intellectuals in that country by 1911. The overpopulation psychology that we are now being exposed to here began to develop there at that time. After their defeat in World War I, there was a collapse of social and moral values in Germany (just as we are experiencing here) and abortion, although still illegal, became rampant. The euthanasia movement against worthless people was launched about 1920. By the time Hitler came, the stage was set, and his first program in mass killing was able to take place only because of what had happened as abortion had become an accepted thing. Hitler exterminated 275,000 people—not Jews, but the frail, the infirm, and the retarded. Eventually, as World War II approached, amputees from World War I were eliminated because they were of no service to the Reich.[99]

What can we expect from a society that can rationalize away the most fundamental of human values, the value of life? What will become of us if we permit society, through the courts, to legalize murder as a solution to a personal problem? Our problems are great because we fight perverted power in high places. The Rockefeller Commission, the Ford Foundation, the Sunnen Foundation, and the Scaife Foundation are all heavily involved in pushing abortion and those things which follow it as inevitably as night follows day. The Rockefeller Commission, for example, recommended not only abortion but sex education and contraceptives for teen-agers without parental consent, subsidized family planning services for all, widespread sterilization of males and females, and government subsidized child care centers for all families wishing to make use of them.[100] Is this very far from Hitler's Germany?

Hear what your children might well read in their college biology textbook (*Life on Earth,* by Wilson, et al): "Abortion is the most effective method of population control... At what point a fetus becomes a human being is a controversial, biological, and ethical question. The moral dilemma is further complicated by the knowledge that in many cases a particular fetus will be seriously defective or unwanted by its parents. Born with such a handicap a child is likely to lead a troubled life and to add a heavy burden on an already overpopulated society... Abortion has always been one of the most popular methods of birth control throughout the world." [101] Magnificent misrepresentation spoken with great authority.

In the book *Human Ecology, Problems and Solutions*, by Paul and Anne Ehrlich (1973)[102] the following statement on page 235 is significant in reference to the brainwashing that takes place in academic publications. "The fetus given the opportunity to develop properly before birth and given the essential early socializing experiences and sufficient nourishing food during the crucial years after birth will ultimately develop into a human being." One of the best proper ways to develop before birth is to be free of the attention of an abortionist! Indeed, it is an entirely new idea that if you are given good food after birth you will *ultimately* develop into a human being.

Dr. Bernard Nathanson writing on two separate occasions for the *New England Journal of Medicine* had these things to say: "One feature that distinguishes the center (in which Dr. Nathanson worked in New York) from all other hospitals and abortion facilities is the use of the individual pre-abortion counseling. The counselor is a college-educated young woman, twenty-one years of age or older, who has had at least one induced abortion. She has been carefully screened for qualities of warmth and concern, in addition to intelligence and efficiency." [103] How delightful that Dr. Nathanson provides not only a woman with the remarkable maturity of twenty-one years but one who has had at least one abortion as the counselor for his disturbed patient. Dr. Nathanson's second quotation: "I am deeply troubled by my own increasing certainty that I had in fact presided over 60,000 deaths. There is no longer serious doubt in my mind that human life exists within the womb from the very onset of pregnancy... Life ... is a continuous spectrum that begins in utero and ends at death. The bands of that spectrum are designated by words such as fetus, infant, child, adolescent, and adult."[105] In spite of what Dr. Nathanson wrote in 1974 (and remember, he thought he presided over 60,000 deaths), he still believes that there should be no law regulating abortion.

When Mrs. Finkbine had her abortion in Sweden as an act of compassion in 1962, abortion was illegal in Sweden. By strange contrast, by January 1, 1975, every doctor in Sweden became obliged to perform abortions on any woman requesting one during the first trimester, under threat of a jail sentence. So we went, in Sweden, from illegal abortion, even for a cause such as Mrs. Finkbine's, to the point of not only abortion on demand, but on demand under threat of jail sentence if the physician refused.[105]

Incidentally, a follow-up on Mrs. Finkbine in 1975 indicated that she had become divorced and remarried in 1973. She was quoted as saying that she was learning to deal with guilt, bitterness, and other "leftover feelings."[106]

In Oslo, Norway, eleven student nurses were denied a request to be exempt from assisting during abortions performed under the National Board of Health. The Norwegian Health Director said: "It is an open question if health personnel thus pronouncing a moral condemnation of a certain group of patients can have a place in our health system."[107]

Another attitudinal question arises around the strange use of the word "life." Many have great concern for those who die in war, for those who die as punishment for capital crime, but have no concept that the beating heart that is stopped by the electric chair or the bullet is the same beating heart that is stopped by the abortionist's curette.

Just to mention a few of the anti-life bits of legislation that have cropped up, in Ohio a bill was presented providing compulsory birth control for all female welfare recipients. In Wisconsin a bill was proposed which would force doctors to perform abortions under pain of revocation of their licenses. In Oregon a bill was introduced that would require all hospitals, without exception, to perform abortions and sterilizations. In Illinois there is a bill before the legislature requiring that hospitals be forced to try to save all infants aborted alive even though the original purpose was to kill them. And in Florida, Representative Sackett's bill which was called "Death with Dignity" and was defeated in May of 1973 also included a provision for killing babies after birth.

WHERE ARE WE NOW?

In February 1974 Justice Blackmun said that the decision on abortion he wrote a year ago "will be regarded as one of the worst mistakes in the Court's history or one of its greatest decisions, a turning point." He also stated that the abortion ruling was "a case the Court couldn't win because the country is so evenly divided on the subject."[108]

It is said that social reform seldom moves backward. The only way that the horror I have been recounting can be corrected is by a constitutional amendment which pro-scribes abortion. It can be done; it will take a tremendous united effort. Remember that it was only the indignant pro-test of concerned citizens that eliminated the indiscriminate use of the living, unborn and born human fetus in scientific experimentation. The fact that the conscience of American people, working through the pro-life movement, brought about this change is historically significant and should not be discounted or minimized.

There has been a reaction in some states to attempt to enact laws which would protect the unborn baby in some way without running into the decision of the Supreme Court. Pennsylvania's legislators, for example, passed what seemed like a very reasonable bill stipulating that a minor child could not have an abortion without her parents' consent nor could a woman have an abortion without the baby's father's consent. The governor promptly vetoed the bill and the veto was overridden by a large margin. The bill has since been declared to be unconstitutional.

The Rhode Island Superior Court in Providence on June 20, 1974, reported the following from the decision of Justice Bulman: "The uncontradicted evidence, exceptionally well prepared and presented by plaintiffs, establishes that:

1. Human life begins at the moment of conception, i.e., at the moment the female egg is fertilized by the male sperm.
2. Induced abortion does not constitute good medical care but to the contrary is a destructive procedure, pregnancy being not a state of disease but a normal condition.
3. Abortion is harmful to public health in Rhode Island.
4. Abortion is harmful to the health of the mother, both physical and mental.
5. Abortions have long-term bad effects on both mother and later unborn children.
6. Legal abortion neither reduces nor eliminates "illegal" (i.e., clandestine) abortions and may increase them.
7. Seldom if ever is there psychiatric indication for aborting the woman."[109]

I would agree with all this but not confine the pertinence to Rhode Island.

In November 1975 the Illinois legislature, overriding the governor's veto, legislated: "If those decisions of the United States Supreme Court ever reverse or modify or the United States Constitution is amended to allow protection of the unborn, then the former policy of this state to prohibit abortions unless necessary for the preservation of the mother's life shall be reinstated.''[110]

While the well meaning groups which I support continue their roles as educator, moral conscience, and prophetic witness, they and we must all turn some attention to alternatives to abortion so that the choice is not abortion or "go through with it." The pregnant woman who is frightened, unmarried, lonely, despondent, etc., should be able to turn to those with compassion for her state with the expectancy that she will be protected, counseled, provided for, and that her unwanted child will be properly placed in a sincerely wanting home.

Abortion is the least that we can offer to a pregnant woman who for any one of a variety of reasons does not see her way clear to having a baby. Here lies the challenge— especially the Christian challenge as an alternative to abortion. Parenthetically, let me say that since the liberalization of abortion there are countless childless couples who no longer are able to adopt from the pool of what were formerly unwanted but born human beings.

If the Supreme Court's decision is not reversed by a constitutional amendment which is pro-life, and the right to an abortion is therefore continually upheld, one can predict without question what will be the Supreme Court's action someday in reference to euthanasia. Obvious among the factors which would favor a decision for euthanasia is the fact that the person concerned, namely the "victim" of euthanasia, is able himself to make a decision—in contrast to the unborn child, who needs an advocate. One wonders in looking ahead if we will not have a new profession, namely the agent of the euthanasia decision. He could well become the counterpart of the executioner of days gone by.

The legalization of abortion-on-demand in the United States, if it is not reversed, will someday be looked upon by historians as the last turning point of a materialistic society in abandoning the advantages accruing to our society from a Judeo-Christian heritage in favor of a change in our culture where an unreal concern about overpopulation has replaced our traditional view of the sanctity of life. Regardless of one's spiritual understanding, his religion, or his faith, when he abandons the sanctity of human life in the unborn state, he seeks to live in harmony with a materialistic society that has permitted itself to be brainwashed to the point where words no longer have their original meaning. He has permitted expediency to replace natural law if he can tolerate the madness of abortion to avoid the inconvenience of pregnancy.

Dean Joseph O'Meara of Notre Dame Law School feels that the abortion cases will be reversed. I trust he is right but I have great doubt that it can be accomplished as he outlines it, but rather it will take an almost superhuman effort to bring about a constitutional amendment: "The abortion cases have settled nothing. They are so full of contradictions and *non sequiturs,* so lacking in any basis in the Constitution or prior cases, that they cannot stand. Even those who, for whatever reason, advocate abortion must deplore the Court's shoddy performance, devoid of judicial craftsmanship, in those inexcusable cases.... Sooner or later they will be reversed, expressively or subsalencio."[111]

Abortion is such an apparently easy way out for so many things. It rids the woman of the necessity of going through a pregnancy which she does not want. It takes care of other social problems such as illegitimacy of a child and an unwed mother. It has the insidious support of a certain part of the medical profession because it is a very lucrative part of obstetrics and particularly so when (partly because of it) the live birth rate is going down. It is also such an easy way out if people are undisciplined in their practice of contraception or if contraception properly practiced fails.

You may be made to feel that if you oppose abortion you somehow or other have missed joining the mainstream of intellectual opinion. You may have to apologize for the stand that you take before taking it. Unfortunately, because society puts you in this position, it remains for you to prove your point rather than for your opponents to prove theirs.

It should be obvious that as soon as one questions the value of human life there really is nothing to prevent him from considering what human beings under what circumstances should rightfully be exterminated. It takes almost nothing to move from abortion, which is the killing of an unborn baby in the uterus, to the killing of the retarded, the crippled, the sick, the elderly.

Take heed, you who do not fit into someone's ecological ideal in form and function. That day may not be very far off when a death selection committee declares that you are no longer a person.

I can think of no better thought to leave with you than that expressed by Malcolm Muggeridge, widely acclaimed British author for the past forty-five years. His concern about abortion was expressed in the London *Sunday Times* and was slightly abridged in *The Human Life Review*.[112]

"Can it be seriously contended that the mere circumstance of being delivered transforms the developing embryo from a lump of jelly with no rights of any kind, and deserving of no consideration of any kind, into a human being with all the legal rights that go therewith? In the case of the pregnant woman injured in a motor accident, damages can be claimed on behalf of the child in her womb. Similarly, in the U. N. declaration of rights of the child, special mention is made of its entitlement to pre- as well as postnatal care. It is a strange sort of prenatal care which permits the removal of the child from its mother's womb, to be tossed into an incinerator, or used for 'research,' or rendered down for cosmetics.

"Our western way of life has come to a parting of the ways; time's take-over bid for eternity has reached a point at which irrevocable decisions have to be taken. Either we go on with the process of shaping our own destiny without reference to any higher being than man, deciding ourselves how many children should be born, when and what varieties, which lives are worth continuing and which should be put out, from whom spare parts—kidneys, hearts, genitals, brain boxes even—shall be taken and to whom allotted.

"Or we can draw back, seeking to understand and fall in with our Creator's purpose for us rather than to pursue our own; in true humility praying, as the founder of our religion and civilization taught us, Thy will be done.

"This is what the abortion controversy is all about and what the euthanasia controversy will be about when as must inevitably happen soon, it arises. The logical sequel to the destruction of what are called 'unwanted children' will be the elimination of what are called 'unwanted lives'—a legislative measure which so far in all human history only the Nazi government has ventured to enact.

"In this sense, the abortion controversy is the most vital and relevant of all. For we can survive energy crises, inflation, wars, revolutions and insurrections, as they have been survived in the past; but if we transgress against the very basis of our mortal existence, becoming our own gods and our own universe, then we shall surely and deservedly perish from the earth."

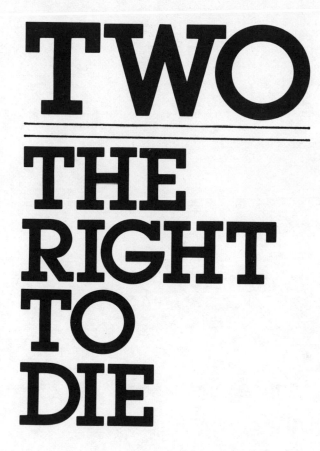

TWO

THE RIGHT TO DIE

In this bicentennial year we are constantly reminded of the words of Thomas Jefferson[1] concerning the inalienable rights of man to life, liberty, and the pursuit of happiness. But we recognize that the definition of life, the definition of liberty, and the definition of pursuit of happiness can raise many moral and ethical dilemmas, especially as we attempt to interrelate these rights. These terms eventually defy full definition.

The process of death is a pinpoint in time for some, a short episode in life for others, and a seemingly endless transition for still others. The brevity of the first is frequently considered to be a blessing for the recipient and a tragedy for those who are left behind. The last is considered to be a tragedy for both recipient and observer. Part of this has to do with the failure of our culture to recognize death as part of the process of life which begins before birth. Death is believed by some to be a step into oblivion—the end of everything. At the other end of the scale it is a step from temporal life to eternal life. For a great host of people it is something more vague between these two possibilities. In any event, for most people it represents the ultimate in the unknown and therefore for most people is frightening. Even for the Christian who looks forward to eternal life, who believes that to be absent from the body is to be present with the Lord[2], death itself may hold no fear but the process of dying is terrifying.

Even though our culture has not been used to speaking of dying and of death with equanimity, there is a growing tendency—in medicine particularly, but also in certain social contexts—to speak of approaching death or the possibility of dying with a new frankness. Out of the freedoms born of this frankness have come considerations of "the right to die," of "death with dignity," the discussion of a "living will," and the resurrection, for common use, of the term *euthanasia* which formerly was a subject for discussion only among a relatively small group of liberals. The definition of "right" in Webster's *New World Dictionary* in the sense in which it is used here is "that which a person has a just claim to; power, privilege, etc., that belongs to a person by law, nature, or tradition; as 'it was his right to say what he thought.' " The laws and the traditions of our land enunciate a right to life but not a right to death.

A "living will" is a document written by a person during his active life while in sound mind, directing that at the time of approaching death he might be permitted to "die with dignity"—another term that has crept into our language with the freedom of speaking about dying and death. It appears to be a deeply ingrained instinct of man to hang on to life. The most legally foolproof "living will" cannot be expected to hold water necessarily at the time of the approaching death of the world-be testator. Experience has shown that people view death differently when it approaches than they did years before. There are also legal implications of what physicians might do under such "living will" instructions without trespassing upon the law. For example, if a prospective patient were to leave instructions that if he were dying with such-and-such a diagnosis and had come to such-and-such a stage in the process of dying, his physician was to terminate his life, this would be directing a physician to commit homicide. Obviously, the physician could not commit homicide and expect, at this stage of our legal understanding, to be innocent of homicide just because a "living will" directed him to do what he did.

The term *euthanasia* comes from the Greek and means painless, happy death *(eu*—well, plus *thanatos*—death). Webster's dictionary goes on to define euthanasia as "an easy and painless death, or, an act or method of causing death painlessly so as to end suffering: advocated by some as a way to deal with victims of incurable disease." The Euthanasia Society of America, founded in 1938, defines euthanasia as the "termination of human life by painless means for the purpose of ending severe physical suffering." Gradually the meaning of one word changed from the connotation of easy death to the actual medical deed necessary to make death easy. Finally it reached the connotation of "mercy killing." The idea that abortion is not killing is a brand new idea. However, the fact that euthanasia is not killing has really never existed. The common synonym for euthanasia in both lay and professional vocabularies has been mercy killing. In any discussion of euthanasia an understanding of terminology is essential. The deliberate killing of one human being by another, no matter what the motivation might be, is murder. Some distinction is usually made between a positive, decisive, death-producing act and the act of permitting death to occur by withholding life-support mechanism or life-extending procedures which in common parlance might be called heroic and in medical terminology might be called "extraordinary means."

The current discussions of the right to die are, in essence, a broad reflection on the moral and ethical problems created by an understanding of the term *euthanasia*. A consideration of the right to die carries with it the implication of the right of *how* to die. Does a patient have the right to expect a painless, comfortable death? Does he have the right to expect that his physician should see that it is so? Does he have the right to expect that the physician might take an active role in his dying process to shorten it for the sake of the patient's comfort or peace of mind? Does the patient have the right to expect the physician to terminate his life if the physician deems it advisable? Could this ever be an active role on the part of the physician or may he assume only a passive role? Is there a difference between an active and a passive role in this regard; is a deed of omission less reprehensible than a deed of commission legally, ethically, or morally? Does the patient have the right to participate in the decision, or better yet, to influence it?

The way one answers any of these questions will depend a good deal upon his view of life. If he is God-oriented in the sense of being either a conservative follower of Judaism or if he is a Christian, and if he indeed believes that the Scriptures are the Word of God and teach that life is precious to God, he will view life as a holy thing, its end not to be decided upon by man. Yet, many physicians who truly believe that the Scriptures are the Word of God and that they give specific admonitions concerning the sanctity of life, will, in the role of physician, act passively in certain circumstances rather than carry out what the laity might call heroic measures to prolong life.

If, on the other hand, the individual's view of life is atheistic, agnostic, or utilitarian, his decisions about participating in the dying process actively or passively are not so much matters of conscience. In between these two views will probably lie the great majority of people who are faced with this kind of decision-making, either as a privilege or an obligation. Although they might not wish to carry the label of a situational ethicist, they would in general be making decisions on the basis of the situation. The situation would encompass for them the patient's state of health, his alertness, his understanding of what was happening to him, and his spoken desires on the matter. But all these would be in the light of the physician's understanding of that patient's disease and that patient's ability to withstand it at all, to withstand it comfortably, or to succumb to it quickly or slowly. One can already see that several physicians might have completely different points of view in a given situation depending upon their previous knowledge of the disease entity in question but also tempered by their previous experience in similar situations where they had been proven right or wrong or where their ethical decisions were affected by the morality which grows out of experience and contact with repetitive problems.

Another facet that the situational ethicist must deal with is the situation in respect to the patient's family. In many situations, for example, there comes a time when the patient's consideration is essentially out of the picture. The patient may be unconscious, truly comatose, definitely out of pain, and waiting for an inevitable death which may be days, weeks, months, or in rare situations even years away. There are emotional factors to be considered in reference to the family and there are definitely economic factors. There may be times when these economic factors may have far-reaching implications. The financial undergirding for the education of a child, for example, might disappear while an unconscious grandmother has her financial substance eaten up by medical bills. The motivation on the part of a family to see a rapid demise in a dying grandmother would understandably be varied but one can see the obvious temptation for a change in motivation as the aforementioned hypothetical example drags on and on.

Can the physician who is in the business of prolonging life and relieving the suffering of the sick and injured be asked to reverse his role and shorten life even while ministering to the needs of the suffering? How much credence should he give to the pressures of the family to terminate life? How can he sort out the motivation that leads to the request? How can he balance his obligation to his patient against his compassion and his understanding for the family? If the right to live and the whole question of killing an unborn baby in the womb raises multiple dilemmas, they are as nothing compared to the dilemmas that are inherent in the question of the right to die.

EUTHANASIA

Before there is any discussion of euthanasia for laymen, it should be medically stated that although death seems imminent to a physician and although he knows it is impossible to turn it away with the armamentarium at his disposal, death can never be exactly predicted as to time. The earlier in the death process one attempts to make this prediction, the less accurate are his prophecies. Yet this does not mean that on the day of death it is necessarily easier to say it will come at 2 o'clock, not at 4, than to say a month in advance it will be in 21 days, not 30.

Secondly, because euthanasia has been, in a sense, a subject which is taboo in our culture and because euthanasia was a term applied by the Nazis to the elimination of those considered to be of no worth to the Reich, we have to separate carefully the various types of euthanasia that one might be talking about. There is a sense in which euthanasia can be construed to mean enabling the patient to die comfortably and/or quickly. It might be said that: 1) a physician could enable a patient to die without quickening his demise, 2) that he could enable a patient to die by removing any barriers to death, 3) that he could enable a patient to die while his motivation was to relieve suffering and 4) a physician could enable a patient to die by taking a deliberate action that would shorten or terminate his life. Other terminology that would describe what I have tried to state here without putting labels in the wrong place would be *direct* or *indirect euthanasia* or *active* or *passive euthanasia.*

If euthanasia means to die happily, then enabling a patient who is going to die to do so happily might include such a thing as administering oxygen to a patient who is in respiratory distress, giving a pain killer in moderate dosage that would not affect the duration of life, or could even be construed to mean giving emotional or spiritual support to the patient by the assurance of care for him or for his loved ones left behind.

Enabling a patient to die by permitting him to die means withholding something that would be considered by most people to prolong the dying life. An example might be to withhold a blood transfusion from a patient with sudden hemorrhage from the stomach, whose death from cancer of the stomach is known to be a very short time away. To withhold a transfusion which could prolong life would be enabling the patient to die by permitting him to die from the "natural" causes that were taking place in the form of his hemorrhage. Although withholding the transfusion might be the action taken by the great majority of physicians, it is possible that in a given circumstance the physician could be held responsible for not doing what he could, for being negligent in the performance of his medical duties; to withhold the transfusion could even be considered manslaughter or possibly homicide.

Enabling a patient to die by a medical act, the motivation of which was the relief of suffering but which had a secondary or side effect of shortening life, could be exemplified by the giving of morphine to a patient, dying in great pain, in spite of the fact that he would require increasingly large doses of morphine with increasing frequency to render him comfortable in order to die "happily." The side effect might be a lethal dose to bring about relief from pain. It is almost unthinkable that a physician with this motivation could be accused of negligence.

Finally, enabling death by a medical act deliberately intended to shorten life, could in the minds of some be closely associated with enabling a patient to die by permitting him to die. The obvious example here is a deliberate overdose of something like morphine, designed to bring an end to a patient's life. Although certain physicians, in recent controversies, have, without naming patients, admitted to repeatedly performing active euthanasia of this sort, I suspect that if one were to analyze dying situations this is not a common procedure in America. If it is, I suspect that because of the fear of eventual malpractice claims or more specifically criminal charges based on manslaughter and homicide laws, physicians would not discuss this with the family, perhaps even when the family has instructed him to so behave. The doctor might, under certain circumstances, have a tacit agreement with his patient to act actively or passively in this regard, or, in other circumstances, he might, out of compassion, act this way without discussion except in his own conscience.

All of the aforementioned examples of enabling death are in general not even considered by doctors or laymen to be under the guise of euthanasia with the exception of the fourth example of enabling a patient to die by deliberately shortening his life. There would seem to be no question about the active participation of the physician here in producing death, presently considered to be a crime.

Quite different in the minds of some is actively or passively participating in the termination of a life of a newborn infant that is not considered worthy to live. One of the best examples of this was the report in the *New England Journal of Medicine*[3] indicating that out of 299 babies who died at the Yale New Haven Hospital in the previous two-and-one-half years, forty-three of them had been allowed to die after the physician had discussed with the family the propriety of not letting the child live. An example—letting a baby with mongolism and intestinal obstruction starve to death rather than giving him life by operating and relieving the obstruction. Whether or not two parties (e.g., the family and the doctor) agree upon active participation or passive participation in any program which will cause the death of an individual is not the issue. It does not change the fact that the motivation was to kill no matter how one explains the deed in terms of compassion and empathy. The least part either party could play in the charge of homicide is accessory before the fact. If one considers all of the possible diagnoses that currently could fall into this category, to say nothing of what could happen if these compassion-motivated tendencies were permitted to go unbridled toward the development of a perfect or super race, it is a specter difficult to contemplate. Children with such obvious diagnoses as Down's syndrome (mongolism), spina bifida (cleft spine) with neurologic changes in lower extremities or in the sphincteric control of bladder and rectum, children with congenital medical illness (such as cystic fibrosis, heralded in the newborn period occasionally by the complicaton of intestinal obstruction), can lead rapidly to the elimination of mentally ill individuals who are considered to be incurable, burdensome, expensive, those brain damaged after injury, senile, etc. Finally, perhaps in the not too distant future, there could be termination of life that is considered unworthy not because of physical or mental incapacity but because of what might be considered to be unworthy life in the field of ethnic origin, economic capacity, political activity, productivity potential, or any other form or function currently considered to be undesirable.

In reference to what might be called passive euthanasia by some but, in a sense, really is not, it should be clearly understood that for most of my association with medicine (thirty-eight years) many physicians have elected not to use artificial life-support mechanisms on dying patients who

they thought were not salvagable. Herein lies the rub—
some who were thought not to be salvagable possibly
were and hence were lost, but this cannot be proven. Others
who were thought to be salvagable in a short period are not;
one is left with a living patient whose life is considered
essentially to be subhuman (see later discussion on Karen
Quinlan).

EXTENSION OF HUMAN LIFE

Probably nowhere in the development of medical technological advances has our ability been greater than in the
specific area of the prolongation or extension of human life
almost at the will of the physician. The life-support systems
which are available in almost any intensive care unit attest
to this fact. It has always been far easier to exterminate life
quite painlessly than to prolong it. The medical profession
now has a two-edged sword: the extension of human life by
artificial means and the painless termination of life by drugs.
The ability of man to wield this sword has moral and ethical
as well as practical considerations that are mind boggling.

Whenever a discussion centers around dying and the
shortening of life, the antithesis of this, namely, the prolongation of life, must be considered. Technologically, medicine
has advanced so quickly that older, unwritten understand-
ings of "ordinary" and "extraordinary" care no longer
seem applicable. What might have been considered "extraordinary" care a few years ago is now so commonplace
as to be called "ordinary" (respirators, pacemakers, kidney
dialysis machines, etc.). Furthermore, what starts off in a
given case to be "ordinary" care such as the application of a
respirator to a patient who is unable to breathe, turns out,
when it becomes evident that the patient never can assume

normal respirations on his own, to have been "extraordinary care," if one is permitted the liberty of changing the adjective after the fact. Perhaps an example would help to clarify this. If one were struck down by a car and had a serious head injury which rendered him unable to breathe and made him unable to respond, and if his bladder sphincter were in spasm so that he could not urinate, he could be placed on a respirator, he could be artificially fed intravenously or by a stomach tube, and his urinary obstruction could be taken care of by the proper placement of a catheter. If it were assumed that he would recover in a matter of a few days, all of these things would be "ordinary" care. If on the basis of superior knowledge of the neurosurgeon attending him at this time it were known that there was essentially no way he could be expected to recover, all of these things might be considered "extraordinary" care, since without them his injuries would produce death.

If one had acute appendicitis and postoperatively developed a situation where his kidneys did not function, to put him on a dialysis machine (an artificial kidney) which could handle his urinary function temporary would be an extraordinary act and might at times be considered to be "extraordinary" care. However, in a vigorious, alert, productive individual with a normal life expectancy of several decades ahead of him, it should not be considered "extraordinary" care. On the other hand, if in a 90-year-old individual the same kidney shutdown took place and was the result of a disease process that inevitably would take this patient's life, the institution of dialysis would be an "extraordinary procedure" and would definitely be thought of, by any medically competent individual, as providing "extraordinary" care. Here the difference perhaps is less difficult to ascertain than in the previously mentioned case of head injury.

To show how difficult predictions might be, *Medical*

World News on May 5, 1974, reported a case of a woman with myasthenia gravis who lived "artificially" for 652 days in intensive care and then made a remarkable recovery. Said a hospital representative at the Harbor General Hospital in Torrance, California, "She made us recognize that there was no such thing as an inordinate effort. She had such a tenacity for life we felt that everything we did, no matter how extraordinary, was appropriate to the situation."[4]

As will be shown subsequently in a discussion of the dilemma raised by the legal trial concerning Karen Quinlan, it is most difficult to judge medical action from the standpoint of what is legal justice alone. If one gets into the pure aspects of ethics, there could be concern that the use of a pain killer in a dying individual could so cloud his conscious response that he might not in his dying moments be in a position to make decisions which in theological terms might bear upon his eternal destiny. It is essentially impossible to control pain in most instances, particularly in a debilitated or dying individual, without at the same time temporarily impairing his ability to think. From a purely ethical point of view, because clouding of judgment accompanies relief from pain produced by drugs, the situation seems to be insurmountable and therefore has become acceptable.

With the technological advances in medicine, the opportunities for physician participation in momentous decisions concerning life and death increase dramatically. But so do the temptations to misuse this newfound expertise. The physician of a generation or two ago was practically powerless to extend life but on the other hand he faced fewer dilemmas.

Helmut E. Erhart[5] has outlined the history of euthanasia societies and euthanasia movements after World War I. He notes that in Germany "mentally dead children" or "monsters" and "hopelessly" insane adults were included in consideration for euthanasia. The British Euthanasia Society, on the other hand, from the beginning and without alteration in their program, has limited itself to "assistance in dying with deliberate shortening of life" in the legal sense of killing on request and has concentrated its efforts on this. In America, the original program of the Euthanasia Society also took up the problem of involuntary euthanasia by including "hopelessly defective infants." However, soon the United States followed the course or pattern in England, which in the mind of Erhart was probably the correct perception, that there would be much greater legal difficulties involved in sanctioning involuntary euthanasia which logically would also have to be extended to the "hopelessly handicapped," old, and mentally sick.

The mercy killing referred to in Chapter 2 which took place in the Netherlands certainly was not lawful but it was obviously approved by large segments of the population. The Dutch Health Service has now proposed new guidelines which have been confirmed by the Royal Society for the Promotion of Medical Science.[6] These guidelines allow, in the case of the incurably ill, certain measures of euthanasia "when the process of dying has begun and death is to be expected in the forseeable time." But who really knows?

Very few legal cases against doctors come to attention because they have performed euthanasia. To my knowledge, no doctor has ever been convicted for performing euthanasia. Even when nonmedical people take part in a mercy killing, the courts are usually lenient with such individuals.

DILEMMAS FOR DOCTORS AND LAYMEN ALIKE

The dilemmas presented by euthanasia are not dilemmas for the medical profession alone. They are dilemmas for laymen as well. The situation is somewhat akin to the remarks that are made about the malpractice crisis in American medicine today. Many people say: "The doctors certainly have a difficult problem." The fact of the matter is that it is the patient who has a difficult problem. Who do you suppose will pay for the doctor's malpractice insurance premium which has increased in cost fivefold? You, the patient, will pay that. What other dangers exist for the patient in an era where the specter of malpractice suits hangs over the head of the responsible physician at all times? First of all, the physician will treat you not on the basis of what his experience and learned intuition dictates, but rather he will do those things which he feels would absolve him from eventual guilt were he ever sued, and he will neglect to do those things which you might need but which involve a high risk concerning a malpractice. In short, the patient's physician must practice defensive medicine and the loss is not only the physician's, it is the patient's.

So it is in the dilemmas surrounding euthanasia. Sooner or later you, the reader, will have to face some of these questions in reference to a member of your family and eventually your family will have to face these questions in reference to you. Indeed, you may be party to the latter dilemma as you approach the end of your life.

Once any one category of human being is considered fair game in the arena of the right to life, where does it stop? If the mongoloid is chosen as the first category whose life is not worthy to be lived, what about the blind and the deaf? If the hopeless cripple confined to a wheelchair and considered to be a burden on society is the first category to be chosen, what about the frail, the retarded, and the senile? It does not take much fanciful imagination to extend these categories to include certain categories of disease such as cystic fibrosis, diabetes, and a variety of neurologic disorders. The population-control people who are concerned about food supply have been very effective in influencing society's thinking on abortion; it seems very logical that eventually one of their targets could be the obese individual who not only has eaten too much already but has to eat a lot to sustain his large body.

It is very easy to slip into moral deception in a discussion of euthanasia. One starts from the point of view of abortion and says, "I can see why you are against abortion because after all someone, preferably the law, must protect the fetus because the fetus is not in a position to protect itself. But when one is talking of euthanasia, if the person is willing to undergo a 'mercy killing,' why should other people object?" The answer is really the same as it is for abortion. Abortion-on-demand opens up other abuses of which euthanasia is number one. Euthanasia opens up the opportunity at this early stage of the game for almost inconceivable fraud, deception, and deceit. Think of the burdensome elderly people, economically burdensome, whose rapid demise could be looked upon as an economic blessing for their family. Think of the temptation to hasten a legacy. Think of how easy, when there are ulterior motives, to emphasize the surcease from suffering and anxiety that comes with painless death.

PRACTICAL
CONSIDERATIONS

I don't think a medical student is ever told what his mission in life is. Certainly no one told me when I was a medical student what was expected of me as a lifetime goal in assuming the role of a physician. Yet it is very clearly and indelibly imprinted upon the mind of the physician that the first obligation toward his patient is to heal him and cure him and to postpone death for as long a time as possible. The second goal is more difficult to enunciate and ever so much more difficult to practice: when cure is not possible the physician is to care for and comfort his dying patient. There is in here a gray area where the physician is not certain about the possibility of cure and yet is not ready to treat the patient as one who needs comfort in dying. The other side of that coin has to do with the behavior of the physician who, realizing that the opportunity for cure is passed, has two options: first, that of maintaining the life of a "dying" patient through the extremely difficult times of transition from active life to inactive life and from inactive life to death, or, secondly, to withhold certain supportive measures which would enable nature to take her course more quickly.

Let me illustrate. There is a unique tumor of childhood called the neuroblastoma in which I have been interested for more than thirty years. Because of this I have developed a broad clinical experience with the behavior of this tumor as it affects the lives of my patients and I have perhaps had more neuroblastoma patients referred to me than would normally be the case, because of my special interest in this tumor. I present this background in order to establish the fact that with this particular tumor I have considerable expertise in understanding the clinical course and have been able to predict with relative accuracy what will happen in a given patient when certain signs and symptoms occur or when certain responses to treatment are known. In a given situation I might have as a patient a five-year-old child whose tumor was diagnosed a year ago and who, in spite of all known treatment, has progressed to a place where although her primary tumor has been removed she now has recurrence of the tumor (metastases) in her bones. On the basis of everything I know by seeing scores of patients like her I know that her days of life are limited and that the longer she lives the more likely she is to have considerable pain. She might also become both blind and deaf, because those are sequelae that might be expected when this tumor spreads in the bones of the skull.

If this five-year-old youngster is quite anemic, her ability to understand what is happening to her might be clouded. If her normal hemoglobin level should be 12 and it is now 6, I have two choices. I can let her exist with a deficient hemoglobin level knowing that it may shorten her life but also knowing that it will be beneficial in the sense that she will not be alert enough to understand all that is happening around her. On the other hand I could be a medical purist and give her blood transfusions until her hemoglobin level was up to acceptable standards. In the process of so doing she would become more alert, she would be more conscious of the things happening around her, she would feel her pain more deeply, and she might live longer to increase the problems presented by all of these things.

In the second place there are anticancer drugs which I know beyond any shadow of a doubt will not cure this child, but which may shrink the recurring tumor in several parts of her body, postponing the inevitable death by a matter of a few days or weeks. However, it is possible that the effect of these drugs will not be very dramatic on the tumors in the skull. They may relentlessly expand, producing blindness and deafness. Would it be better to let this little girl slip into death quietly, with relatively little pain, and with her parents knowing that she can both see and hear—or should we prolong her life by two or three weeks, increase the intensity and duration of the pain she would have, and possibly run the risk of the added terrible complications for the family to witness: blindness and/or deafness? In such a circumstance I opt to withhold supportive measures that would prolong miserable life for the patient to bear and the family to see.

I well remember the occasion on which I decided that this would always be my course of action in this particular tumor unless I was forced to do otherwise or there were some very extenuating circumstances. One of my patients was approaching the aforementioned condition and had been sent home because of the approach of the Christmas holidays and the desire of his family to have the child with them. In the days before his discharge I had promised him a chemistry set as a Christmas gift and on the day before Christmas I delivered the gift in the afternoon. His family took me into their living room and there before the Christmas tree was a big mound on the floor which looked like a heaped-up beige blanket. Under it was my patient on his hands and knees slumped down as though hands and knees could no longer support his weight. The story was most pitiful. Earlier he had asked to come down from his bedroom to see the electric trains under the Christmas tree and found a measure of comfort on his hands and knees before the trains. He asked not to be moved because he had found a position in which he seemed more comfortable than when lying in bed. He died the next day in that same position.

In a situation such as I have just described one gets to the very nonlegalistic moral core of the relationship of a physician with his patient. Whether the patient is a child and the relationship has to be with his parents or whether the patient is an adult and the physician's relationship must be with the patient himself and his relatives, there has to be a sense of trust and confidence that the physician will do the "right" thing whether the disease process is curable or is one which will cause death. There have been many occasions in my life when I have clearly described the thoughts that went through my mind as I outlined to parents why I planned what I did plan to do with their child. But much more often than that there has been between parent and physician an understanding which exceeds the bounds of pure trust and confidence, where the family seems to know, and I encourage them to think, that their child is in understanding hands as well as in competent hands, that their child will be kindly treated in this terrible process of dying to which death brings a sense of relief and release. Here the family senses that I will treat their child the way I would like someone in my position to treat my child were he in the same circumstance. Yet through all this there is the understanding that this life, waning through it may be, is precious to the patient, is precious to the family, is precious to me, and—in my particular belief—the understanding that this life is also precious to God.

Therefore, it should be very clear that the decisions that are made in any circumstance are tailored to the problems at hand, the background and experience of the physician, the depth of understanding of the family, and the relationship which exists between patient and physician and family and physician. There is no way that there can be a set of rules to govern this circumstance. Guidelines may be possible, but not rules. I can think of no more tragic circumstance to come upon the practice of medicine and no more tragic circumstance for a future patient to face than to have a legal decision made by someone in the field of jurisprudence who has not lived through these circumstances, and who could not in a lifetime of testimony understand what the problems are and how they should be handled. His training, his experience, and his emotions have not been intimately involved with similar circumstances in the past where his decision and his decision alone is the one that must answer all the questions, no matter how inadequately.

The arrival of the era of organ transplantation adds other series of dilemmas to the practice of medicine in reference to the ethics and the morality of the prolongation of life on the one hand or its extermination on the other. Add to all of the other questions that have been raised previously, the new one of terminating one life to make possible an organ transplant to another individual in order that the second individual's life may be meaningfully prolonged. Some of these decisions are relatively open and shut, as for example in brain death of an individual, perhaps young, who is kept alive by a respirator in the presence of a functioning heart. But one can also easily imagine the pressures that develop from the family of a patient consigned to death because of the lack of a vital organ, when the patient could have his life significantly prolonged by the removal of that organ from another individual whose life may not be considered by the patient and other interested parties to be worthy of extraordinary care. These pressures are felt especially by those engaged in kidney transplant programs.

THE CASE OF KAREN QUINLAN

The name Karen Quinlan became identified in the autumn of 1975 in the minds of all who are concerned about matters of life and death with the extraordinary possibility of the termination of life becoming a legal matter. In piecing the story together, *Time* Magazine wrote it this way.[7] Karen Ann Quinlan had been born of unknown parents in Pennsylvania and was adopted by Mr. and Mrs. Joseph Quinlan when she was four weeks old. *Time* said that the Quinlans considered her to be a friendly, outgoing girl, a fine skier and swimmer, and one who sang in their church. Karen's friends in high school, from which she graduated in 1972, described her as quiet but popular with the boys. Her employer, who discharged her because of a company cutback in August of 1974, remembered her as a good, hard worker.

Apparently in the last few months of her active life Karen, after losing her job, moved out of her parents' home and into employment and friendships unlike her previous lifestyle. ''... Somewhere along the line, she began experiment-

ing with drugs. Several friends described her as an occa-
sional marijuana user and frequent pill popper who took
'uppers' and 'downers' to suit her moods.''[8]

Time concluded that drugs were probably responsible for
Karen's current condition. On April 14th, apparently de-
pressed, she not only took some tranquilizers but then went
to a bar to celebrate her friend's birthday. After drinking gin
and tonic, she began to "nod out." Friends took Karen
home and put her to bed, where she passed out. It was
realized that she was more than drunk. Attempts were made
to revive her with mouth-to-mouth resuscitation; an ambu-
lance was called. She never regained consciousness.

It is important to recognize from the standpoint of this
book that Karen was then presented as an emergency situation to the local community hospital where, without much
knowledge of what had happened before, the immediate re-
suscitative measures, including the use of a respirator, were
probably begun. To have taken the time in gaining a history
that would have revealed all that is known months later,
would have forfeited the one opportunity Karen's doctors
had to restore her to active life. It is also worth mentioning
that many people presented to the emergency room of a
hospital with the same signs and symptoms are treated
exactly as Karen was and recover, most of those recovering
having their full faculties.

Time reports that Karen's parents kept hoping that she
would recover and were looking for a miracle. Mr. Quinlan's own parish priest feared that Mr. Quinlan was losing
touch with reality in this regard.

Karen had been in a coma since the early morning of April
15, her breathing maintained by a mechanical device called
a respirator. By all accounts reported in *Time,* she had
shriveled into something scarcely human: she weighed only
sixty pounds, was unable to move a muscle, to speak, or to
think. This was the picture presented to the world through

the news media when in September of 1975 the doctors caring for Karen refused Mr. Quinlan's request to pull the electric plug from the respirator, thereby terminating her life. Mr. Quinlan then sued for his child's right to die, putting it in his own religious terms: "In my own mind, I had already resolved this spiritually through my prayers, and I had placed Karen's body and soul into the gentle, loving hands of the Lord... It was resolved that we would turn the machine off."[9]

There were several facts that were not immediately made known in the media and which have never been clarified in the minds of many who have criticized the eventual decision of Superior Court Judge Robert Muir, Jr., when he finally decided on November 10th that the doctors could not disconnect the life-sustaining respirator from Karen Ann Quinlan's body and allow her to die.

The first of these facts was that Karen was alive. The fact that it was reported that she could not move a muscle was not completely true, because she did respond to pain and cried when pinched. Although her electroencephalographic tracing (electrical brain waves) was not normal, it did show electrical activity which in this gray netherland between life and death has been interpreted over and over again by medical experts to indicate that the brain is still alive, even though it may not appear to think or function. Although many of the medical experts appearing as expert witnesses at the trial agreed that Karen was like a child without a brain, nevertheless they insisted that the machine could not be turned off. The consensus was that Karen met none of the medically accepted criteria for determining death. In other words, in spite of her situation she had not had "brain death," which is the legal definition of death in the eight states that have statutes concerning this matter. (New Jersey, where this trial took place, is not one of them.)

The second fact was that although many medical decisions are not to *start* the use of an extraordinary life-support mechanism such as a respirator, once the decision *is* made to start such (I have already indicated that there was really no alternative to this decision at the time Karen was presented to her emergency room physicians), then with a living organism who has not exhibited brain death, to turn off the life-support mechanism is to deliberately produce death. This act is, in the minds of those interested in intricacies of both law and medicine, homicide.

Third, the whole conduct of medical care these days is governed to a large extent by the shadow of malpractice suits hanging over the medical profession. There are lawyers who say there has never been a relationship between a physician and a patient in which they cannot find a cause for a medical malpractice suit. Whereas in days gone by, medical malpractice centered around not practicing medicine in conformity with the standards of the community, now medical malpractice suits are instituted because the result is less than perfect or less than the patient or his family expected in a given encounter with disease or surgery. Obviously, the specter of malpractice litigation hung over the doctors who were requested to disconnect the respirator from the body of Karen Quinlan.

During the trial a number of things were discussed in the press, not only as news reports but in analyses by people both competent and incompetent to make such analyses. It was clear that whereas it can be argued with conviction that there is a right to live guaranteed by our Constitution (but apparently not applicable to the unborn child), there is no "right to die" under that same Constitution. In fact, many legal actions work in the opposite direction. Members of the Jehovah's Witnesses sect have been legally shown not to have the right to refuse a blood transfusion on religious grounds nor to withhold such from a minor who has not reached the age of consent. It is also legal practice for the courts to appoint guardians for children in order that they will be given adequate medical treatment that parents, for multiple reasons, are unwilling to provide.

Franklin Zimring, professor of law at the University of Chicago, put the matter succinctly in reference to the proper place for decisions of this kind to be made: "Some decisions are beyond the law's competence to make with any rigor or confidence in being right."[10]

There was legal eloquence with theological overtones from such competent and respected jurists as Ralph Porzio, who is not new to these concerns, having written a book in recent years concerning the multitudinous problems of life and death which arise around the medical transplantation of organs from one person to the other. He asked these questions:

"Dare we defy the undisputed premise, the granite foundation of this case, that Karen Ann Quinlan is legally and medically alive?"

"Dare we defy nature's immutable command to survive?"

"Dare we defy the divine command, 'Thou shalt not kill'?"[11]

Many analysts tried to condense into one newspaper column a synthesis of religious and moral teaching of the three major religions in the United States: Judaism, Catholicism, and Protestantism. All of these fell short of anything like reaching the mark because there is no monolithic theological or religious teaching about this matter in any of these religions. What may be the personal, sincere conviction of the Quinlans' parish priest might not be what the Vatican thinks on the same subject. Although Orthodox Judaism has as high a regard for the sanctity of human life based upon the Old Testament Scriptures as can be found in our culture, the younger generation practicing Reform Judaism does not hold to this same high opinion nor does it base its decisions on Scripture. In the Protestant religion, not only are there innumerable denominational differences, but within the denominations both liberal and conservative differences. If one were to ask a situational ethicist such as Joseph Fletcher, he might tell you that death control is the same as birth control. On the other hand an ethicist such as Paul Ramsey, who bases his decisions on the Bible, which he considers to be the Word of God, says it this way: "Attention paid to God's dominion means man has only stewardship over life." And, "Proper stewardship can involve deciding how to live the last days of (one's) life."[12]

I interrupt this train of thought to recall once again to the reader's mind that there is a distinct difference in the mind of the practicing physician who deals with these matters day in and day out between not starting a life support extraordinary technique because he feels it would produce a "Karen Quinlan," and, once having made the decision to start it, terminating it—which is a deliberate act, ending the life of a patient, interpreted by many as homicide.

In mid-November, in a forty-four-page ruling, Judge Robert Muir, Jr., discounted "the compassion, sympathy he felt toward the Quinlan family" and went on to say that both "judicial conscience and morality" told him that Karen's fate was being handled properly by "the treating physician." Under common law, he said, (in spite of) "the fact that the victim is on the threshold of death," no "humanitarian motives" can justify taking life. He dismissed "semantics" by which he referred to questions about whether disconnecting Karen's body from the respirator would be an act of commission or omission. Either would result in the taking of her life, which the law says is homicide. Judge Muir clearly stated that "there is no constitutional right to die that can be asserted by a parent for his incompetent adult child."[13]

It is worthwhile to consider the arguments that were presented by Karen Quinlan's lawyers because they are the arguments that come into the mind of any reader of the press in circumstances that are so reported.

1. "Medical science holds no hope for Miss Quinlan's recovery."

   In fact, doctors at the trial had indicated that there is always a possibility of recovery although not as a human being with cerebral function. The judge concluded that if such were possible, "what level or plateau she will reach is unknown."

2. "Miss Quinlan would want the respirator turned off."

   Mr. Quinlan had stated that his daughter had made statements like this before her concomitant taking of alcohol and drugs somehow put her into the situation which produced her discerebrate condition, causing coma. The judge noted that even if these had been the wishes of Miss Quinlan when she was well and happy it was not when she was "under solemn and sobering fact that death was a distinct choice."

3. "Doctors have no legal obligation to keep Miss Quinlan alive."

   The judge believed that such a duty exists when the physician believes that she should be kept alive. Judge Muir very properly stated that a patient placed in the care of a doctor expects that the doctor "will do all within his human power to favor life against death."

4. "The wishes of the parents of an incompetent patient should be paramount in a doctor's life-or-death decision."

   The judge took a contrary point of view because "there is always the dilemma of whether it is the conscious being's belief or the conscious being's welfare that governs the parental motivation."

5. "The constitutional right of privacy should allow parents or guardians to make the decision that an incompetent child's life should no longer be prolonged."

   Judge Muir believed that all previous right-to-privacy cases concerned rights to maintain a lifestyle, not rights to end life altogether.

6. "Freedom of religion should allow Miss Quinlan, a Roman Catholic, to die."

   Judge Muir felt that the previous interpretations of the right to exercise religious beliefs, as enunciated by the United States Supreme Court, dealt with life on earth, not life hereafter.

7. "The beauty and meaning of Karen's life was over and she should be allowed to die."

   Judge Muir indicated, again rightly so, that nowadays the use of a respirator as an emergency measure in a patient in Karen Quinlan's condition (as it was the night she was presented to the emergency room of the local hospital) was really an ordinary, rather than extraordinary, step in medical practice. He said, "Continuation of medical treatment, in whatever form, where its goal is sustenance of life, is not something degrading, arbitrarily inflicted, unacceptable to contemporary society, or unnecessary."*

In the days that followed Judge Muir's decision, editorial comment in general was in favor of the jurists' point of view and those who knew best about the laws of the land recognized that the laws we now have currently forbid anyone from giving permission to any other person to pull the plug on a life-sustaining machine. The judge knows when he is

*Much of the seven questions have been taken from the excellent analysis of Aaron Epstein, a staff writer of the Philadelphia *Inquirer,* reported in that newspaper November 11, 1975.

asked to give this permission that it is productive of homicide. In that sense, this entire trial was a futile exercise. Somebody should have been able to say at the start that no judge could rightly tell someone else to commit a homicide. After the emotional furor associated with the trial had quieted down, most agreed that the right of Karen to die was not a matter for the courts. This was all well and good, but it opened speculation in another area that could be just as bad.

Most editorial comment, after agreeing that Karen's problem was not a matter for the courts, attributed this to archaic or obsolete laws—and this is wrong. If it were not even called homicide, just to pose an argument, it is impossible for a jurist or, even worse, a jury to make a decision, even when they have all of the pertinent facts such as are available in the case of Karen Quinlan. How then can legislators establish laws on the right to die when Karen Quinlan's problem is only one of literally hundreds that exist, all with different reasons and motivations, and with their attendant emotional overlay?[14]

If well-meaning legislators, pressured by public opinion rising out of the emotional concern around the Karen Quinlan case or others like it, should push several of the United States to formulate laws concerning the right to die, Pandora's box will have been opened to expose a situation that really has no solution. We are dealing with medicine, with technology, and with law. Basic to the relationship between physician and patient is the expectation that life is worthy to be lived, that physicians will act on behalf of their patients toward this end, and that if acts of omission or commission lead to an earlier demise of a patient than might ordinarily have been expected, *these decisions have to remain within the bounds of the expected, compassionate, understanding relationship between the patient and his doctor and the patient's family and the patient's doctor.* The number of examples of this decision-making is legion. It is unthinkable that the law could direct this decision-making on the part of the physician, because to do so would undermine the fundamental principles in all of the great field of health care.

In reviewing a case history like that of Karen Quinlan the decisions are difficult enough and fraught with sufficient danger to give anyone pause even if he confines his attention to concern for the patient and consideration for the patient's family. But since human beings are what they are, if it were possible for the law, in its cold impersonal way, to direct decision-making on the part of a physician concerning life and death, other motives would very quickly enter the picture. Whereas it can be argued that all of the motives in the Karen Quinlan case are pure, the opportunity for base, evil, calculating, conniving motives is wide open if the decision-directed death could be demanded of a physician by way of the law. Without our knowing it, it is the Judeo-Christian concept of the sanctity of human life, even respected by an areligious people, that makes it possible for us to live day by day in the relative security of the obviously imperfect, poorly defined parameters of decision-making concerning death and dying in medicine. To remove the decision-making from the person primarily involved, namely the physician, and to place it in the hands of the law, would remove that security and expose each of us, first, to improper and inappropriate decisions at the time of death. Further, with the erosion of the morality which would necessarily take place, those decisions would be moved closer and closer to vibrant life instead of being confined to the area of waning life.*

*At the time of this writing, a question has been raised concerning Karen Quinlan's condition when she was presented to the emergency room of her community hospital April 15. She had an egg-size bump on her head as well as a series of bruises on her body that had been received shortly before admission (*Time,* December 29, 1975).

THEOLOGY, MORALITY, AND ETHICS

Although the termination of unborn life precludes the living of the life for threescore and ten years, whereas euthanasia only shortens a life that has already been lived, this is no reason to regard the taking of life by euthanasia as any less serious a moral decision than that by abortion.

Obviously, the great majority of people realize that a decision concerning abortion will never be theirs to make personally. It naturally follows that many people will be indifferent to the implications of liberalized abortion laws, not recognizing how the change in our understanding of abortion affects so many other aspects of our lives today and in the future. But when it comes to death, there is no one who can say that a decision concerning the way his death is managed will be of no concern to him. The death rate is still one per capita.

It has always been of considerable interest to me that any discussion of human life rapidly and inevitably becomes associated with theological discussions. The fact that as distinguished a journal as the *Human Life Review* would contain technical articles on population, learned discourses on jurisprudence, and publish them side by side with the theological implications of man's regard for human life suggests to me incontrovertibly that life and death are God's business.

As with abortion, any discussion of euthanasia by the individual leans heavily upon that individual's understanding of the sanctity or lack of sanctity of human life, upon an understanding of man's understanding of God, and upon whether or not in the synthesis of these things the individual believes that there is life not worthy to be lived. My own perspective of the dilemmas presented by euthanasia represent an understanding produced by the synthesis of where my belief in Biblical revelation crosses my experience in medicine.

Each reader of this book must face the fact that his own beliefs on these matters may be based on theological arguments of which he is not aware, as well as on Christian spinoffs that regulate society.

To one raised in Judeo-Christian moral philosophy, life might be considered on a much higher plane than the right considered inalienable by Thomas Jefferson. If one considers life as a sacred privilege, that understanding can be extended to include the view that this sacred privilege was indeed designed by God in order that a creature might relate to the Creator in a personal way—in a relationship in which God is sovereign.

If man was indeed created in the image of God and he was created for a life of fellowship with God, then death is alien to anything that God in his creation of man intended before man's fall. From a theological point of view the sanctity of life represents, or rather understands, man as a trinity: he is a soul, he does inhabit a body, and he has a spirit. In the trinitarian Christian view there is a sanctity of life for each of these.

The term "death with dignity" has caught on because of its alliterative catchiness rather than because it represents anything based upon Judeo-Christian moral principles.[15] The Judeo-Christian understanding of the fall of man is essential to an appreciation of this point of view. Man was created in the image of God and would have lived in fellowship with him, had it not been for the disobedience of the progenitor of our race, Adam. Anything that exists within man's nature to enable him to have fellowship with God must be regarded as a gift from God and, in a sense, the worthiness of this life has meaning only insofar as it has this relationship to God.

In a sense the whole problem of the right to live and the

right to die, centering around one's understanding of abortion and euthanasia, has a significant analogy to the behavior of Lucifer. We do not know whence his temptation came but we do know that he sought to be "like the most high."[16] Our society, having lost its understanding of the sanctity of human life, is pushing the medical profession into assuming one of God's prerogatives, namely, deciding what life shall be born and when life should end.

A great deal of our Western civilization with its concomitant culture is based upon Christian principles, Christian ethics, Christian morality. Even though many refer to this era as the post-Christian era, there are a remarkable number of spinoffs that we accept as everyday rights and privileges which would never have been part of Western society except for Christian influence.

If one were to superimpose a map of the Western world showing those places where the Christian gospel has been preached, where Christian morality and influence has had its greatest impact, upon another map showing those parts of the Western world where what used to be called social reforms were most prevalent—literacy, education, hospitals, orphanages, homes for the aged, institutions for the retarded and the insane available to all regardless of creed—these maps would be almost identical.

Without theological insights that help to form the basis of one's understanding of matters relating to the life and death of patients, I would find it impossible to make judgments in these matters. I suspect that theological principles, some of which may be vague implantations from early religious training, are probably at work in the minds of the great majority of physicians as they face some of these decisions.

If there is not to be a Judeo-Christian ethic in the preservation of life in matters pertaining to euthanasia, what does the future hold? To assume the role of prophet, I can almost hear the arguments that will be given by the proponents of euthanasia outlining the safeguards that the state can build into euthanasia laws to prevent euthanasia from becoming perverted as it once was in the days of the Nazis in Germany. It comes down to the question as it does in reference to any matter of life: "Is there life not worthy to be lived?" The day may come when a death selection committee may objectively consider my life not to be worth much. On the other hand the subjective worth of my life in my eyes and those in my family who love me might be quite different. Many cases will be open and shut, but the number of cases in the gray area will exceed those where physicians have clarity of thought and relative unanimity of opinion. Certainly the rights of individuals will disappear; depersonalization and dehumanization will reign. If our human-value concepts are to be preserved, no one should take the life of another human being even passively without the deepest concern and consideration of all the attendant implications. Once the human-value ethic becomes weakened or tarnished, it doesn't take long for inhuman experimentation on human bodies to take place. Auchwitz could be in the offing.

WHERE DO WE GO FROM HERE?

The decision of the Supreme Court in favor of abortion on demand literally hands over the decision on the survival of one person's life to another person. All of the economic, social, emotional, and compassionate arguments that are used in favor of abortion very suddenly become the same arguments for euthanasia.

It does not take long to move rapidly to a new set of standards once we have learned to live for a short time with an abrogation of a former principle. Take the medical profession, for example. For four centuries longer than the Christian era, doctors have taken the Hippocratic oath. To be sure, there are many things that are outdated because of the difference in culture between the time of Hippocrates and this modern era. To be sure, there are changes in our understanding of modern medicine which alter or render obsolete certain areas of the Hippocratic oath. But the one thing that the public could rely on was that the medical profession, functioning on the traditional oath of Hippocrates, was in the business of being on the side of life. Life was to be preserved just as suffering was to be alleviated. But nowhere were the skills of the physician to be used as intervention to lower the health standards of the patient or to shorten his life.

If the medical profession abandons the life principle embodied in the Hippocratic oath and sees its privilege to extend to the interruption of unborn life in the womb and to painlessly exterminate a waning life much as the veterinarian would put an ailing dog to sleep, it will have changed its *raison d'etre*. The patient can no longer look at his physician as his advocate for the extension of life—because when in the mind of that physician that patient's life is waning, the sick person has no guarantee that the physician will approach him in the role of life preserver; he may be coming as executioner. The medical profession has been disappointingly silent as they have heard the intellectual arguments, Supreme Court rulings, and population-concern pressures that have begun to alter the fundamental basis which has for so long set them apart as the proponents of the healing art.

Before the century is out, it is quite possible that the elderly will exceed in numbers those who bear the burden of their support, whether as family or under some legal technicality such as the Social Security Act. If the question of euthanasia presents a dilemma now, on moral and ethical grounds, think of what it will present in days to come when, in addition to moral and ethical considerations, there is the overpowering question of economics. Unless we get our ethics and our morals straightened out now, the death selection committee that decides for you may be motivated more by money than by ecological concerns.

Most of the dilemmas that present themselves in reference to the dying patient have been described. If the reader feels at this juncture that he does not have a good grasp of how the author would act in every imaginable circumstance, then the reader has grasped the situation rather well. It is almost impossible to present in capsule form how one feels on this subject, so extenuating are the circumstances in different situations. Perhaps no more difficult question is ever asked of me by an intern or a resident than to summarize in a few sentences my feelings on this subject. When asked to do so, I put it somewhat like this: "As a basic principle, keep as many men at as many guns for as long a time as possible; that's how you win the war. I am in the life-saving business and that comes first, but I recognize also that I am in the business of alleviating suffering. I never take a deliberate action with the motive of terminating a patient's life. It is possible that a patient's life might be shortened by some therapeutic measure I employ with the intent of relieving suffering. In some circumstances where I believe that I have sufficient experience and expertise with the life history of a disease process and my patient's response to that disease as well as to his therapy, I might withhold treatment that could be considered extraordinary or heroic in the given circumstance in reference to the quality of life that might be salvaged for a short period of time." Even as I write these words I recognize full well the chance for errors in judgment. Because of that I try to err only on the side of life.

NOTES

INTRODUCTION
  1. 2 Timothy 3:16.

CHAPTER 1
  1. The Declaration of Independence.
  2. Albert Schweitzer, *Civilization and Ethics* (London: A. C. Black, 1946).
  3. D. M. Jackson, *The Sanctity of Life* (London: Christian Medical Fellowship).
  4. H. O. J. Brown, "What the Court Didn't Know," *Human Life Review,* Vol. I, No. 2, 1975.
  5. Brown, "What the Court Didn't Know."
  6. Genesis 4:15.
  7. Genesis 9:5, 6.
  8. Exodus 20:13.
  9. Exodus 21:22.
  10. Matthew 5:17.
  11. John 5:39.
  12. Report of the Joseph P. Kennedy Foundation International Symposium on Human Rights. Retardation and Research, Washington, D. C. The John F. Kennedy Center for the Performing Arts, October 16, 1971.
  13. *Newsweek,* Nov. 12, 1973, page 70.
  14. Psalm 139:12-16.
  15. Isaiah 44:1, 2.
  16. Isaiah 44:24.
  17. Jeremiah 1:5.
  18. Exodus 3:2.
  19. Exodus 4:10.
  20. Exodus 4:11.
  21. L. B. Arey, *Development Anatomy, A Textbook and Laboratory Manual of Embryology,* 7th edition, (Philadelphia: W. B. Saunders, 1965), pp. 85-105.

22. L. M. Hellman, J. A. Pritchard, eds., *Williams' Obstetrics*, 14th edition (New York: Appleton, Century & Crofts, 1971), pp. 1089-91.

B. N. Nathanson, "Suction Curettage for Early Abortions: Experience with 645 Cases," *Clinical Obstetrics and Gynecology*, 14:99-107, 1971.

23. R. C. Benson, *Handbook of Obstetrics and Gynecology* (Los Altos, Calif.: Lange Medical Publishers, 1974), p. 438.

24. Benson, *Handbook of Obstetrics,* p. 1092.

J. M. Mackenzie, A. Roufa, H. M. Lovell, "Midtrimester Abortion: Clinical Experience with Amniocentesis and Hypertonic Instillation in 400 Patients," *Clinical Obstetrics and Gynecology*, 14:107-124, 1971

25. J. Peel, M. Potts, *Textbook of Contraceptive Practice:* Hysterotomy. (Cambridge: University Press, 1969), pp. 197-198.

26. P. G. Stubblefield, "Abortion vs. Manslaughter," *Surgery*, 110:790, 1975.

27. J. R. Stanton, *Abortion: Flawed Premise and Promise,* to be published.

28. *Markle* v. *Able,* Supreme Court of the United States, #72-56, 72-30, p. 72.

29. Newsletter of Americans United for Life, Vol. 2, No. 1, Feb. 1975.

30. U. S. Center for Disease Control, Atlanta, Ga., Vol. 24, No. 3, Jan. 18, 1975.

31. Stanton, *Abortion.*

32. *Terminology Bulletin,* No. 1, September 1965, The American College of Obstetricians and Gynecologists.

33. "Statement on Abortion by 100 Professors of Obstetrics," *American Journal of Obstetrics and Gynecology,* 112:992, 1972.

34. *School District* v. *Shempp,* 374, U. S. 203 (1963).

35. *Miller* v. *California,* 413, U. S. 15 (1973).

36. *Furman* v. *Georgia,* 408, U. S. 238 (1972).

37. United Nations Declaration of the Rights of the Child, November 20, 1959, *Everyman's United Nations,* 8th Ed, (New York: United Nations), p. 360.

38. Supreme Court of the U. S. Syllabus, *Roe et al* v. *Wade,* decided 1-22-73, 410, U. S.

39. Brown, "What the Court Didn't Know."
40. *Roe et al* v. *Wade*, see note 38.
41. J. O'Meara, *Human Life Review*, Vol. 1, No. 4, 1975.
42. O'Meara, *Human Life Review*.
43. *Roe et al* v. *Wade*, see note 38.
44. See Note 38.
45. Declaration of Human Rights
46. *World Medical Association Bulletin*, 1:22, April 1949, p. 22.
47. H. O. J. Brown, "Abortion: Rights or Technicalities?" *Human Life Review*, Vol. 1, No. 3, 1975.
48. See Note 38.
49. *Roe* v. *Wade*, Syllabus, First concurring opinion.
50. N. St. John-Stevas, "On the Firing Line," the TV program (William F. Buckley) taped in New York, March 3, 1975, from *Human Life Review*, Vol. 1, No. 3, 1975 (appendix).
51. 1st International Conference on Abortion, Fall of 1967, Washington, D. C.. Sponsored by Harvard Divinity School and Joseph P. Kennedy, Jr., Foundation.
52. M. J. Sobran, "Rhetoric and Cultural War," *Human Life Review*, Vol. 1, No. 1, page 96, 1975.
53. "A New Ethic for Medicine and Society," an editorial, *California Medicine*, 113:67, 1970.
54. "Birth Crisis in Japan," South Bend *Tribune*, July 26, 1974 (quoted by J. O'Meara in *Human Life Review*, Vol. 1, No. 4, 1975).
55. *Marriage and Family Newsletter*, May-June, 1973.
56. "Birth Crisis in Japan."
57. *Medical World News*, October 12, 1973.
58. *Medical Tribune*, February 5, 1975.
59. H. Stallworthy, _____. Moolgaokeras, and J. J. Walsh, "Legal Abortion: A Critical Assessment of Its Risks," *Lancet*, 1245:1249, 1971.
60. H. O. J. Brown, "A Survey of Legalized Abortion and the Public Health," special report in *Human Life Review*, Vol. 1, No. 3, 1975.
61. H. O. J. Brown, "Abortion: Rights or Technicalities?" *Human Life Review*, Vol. 1, No. 3, 1975, pp. 72, 73.
62. "Zero Pregnancies in 3,500 Rapes," *The Educator*, Vol. 2,

No. 4, September 1970 (quoted in Willke, *Handbook on Abortion*).

63. J. C. Willke, *Handbook on Abortion* (Cincinnati: Holtz and Hayes, 1975), p. 33.

64. Newsletter of Americans United for Life, Vol. 1, No. 1, November 1972.

65. J. Blake, *Science,* 171:540, 1971.

66. *Time* Magazine, October 19, 1972.

67. Newsletter of Americans United for Life, January 1973.

68. Alan F. Guttmacher, "Abortion—Yesterday, Today, and Tomorrow," *The Case for Legalized Abortion Now* (Berkeley, Calif., Diablo Press, 1967).

69. Alan F. Guttmacher, "Therapeutic Abortion: The Doctor's Dilemma," *Journal of Mt. Sinai Hospital,* New York, 21:1954.

70. M. E. Avery, "Consideration on the Definition of Viability," *New England Journal of Medicine*, 292:206, 1975.

71. *Medical World News,* November 9, 1973.

72. *Reader's Digest,* November 1973, p. 144.

73. D. P. Warwich, Hastings Center Report, December 1974.

74. Sobran, "Rhetoric and Cultural War," p. 98.

75. Sobran, "Rhetoric and Cultural War."

76. J. Pakter, D. Harris, F. Nelson, "Surveillance of the Abortion Program in New York City: Preliminary Report, *Clinical Obstetrics and Gynecology,* 14:267-300, 1971.

77. Thomas W. Hilgers and Dennis J. Horan, "The Sexual Revolution Is Yet to Begin," in *Abortion and Social Justice* (New York: Sheed and Ward, 1972), pp. 221-229.

78. Sobran, "Rhetoric and Cultural War."

79. Sobran, "Rhetoric and Cultural War."

80. Congressional Record, Vol. 119, Washington, October 1, 1973. 145 S 18272 to the Foreign Assistance Act, 1973 (S2335).

81. Congressional Record. See Note 80.

82. Congressional Record. See Note 80.

83. Newsletter of Americans United for Life, Vol. 1, No. 5, 1973.

84. *Living,* November-December 1975 (Right to Life of Southern California Newsletter), Vol. 6, No. 4.

85. Newsletter of Americans United for Life, Vol. 2, No. 2, 1975.

86. *Christianity Today,* February 16, 1973, p. 516.

87. H. E. Ehrhardt, "Abortion and Euthanasia, Common Problems," *Human Life Review,* Vol. 1, No. 3, 1975.

88. *Dred Scott* v. *Sandford,* 19 How. 393, 1856.

89. *U. S.* v. *Calley,* 46 CMR 1131 (ACMR) 1973 aff'd, 22 USCMA 534 48 CMR 19 1973.

90. Center for Disease Control, U. S. Department HEW, quoted by Americans United for Life in an advertisement in the *Wall Street Journal,* January 22, 1974.

91. Philadelphia *Evening Bulletin,* May 16, 1973.

92. J. Nadol, "Who Shall Live? Who Shall Be Aborted? Who Shall Reproduce? Who Shall Decide?" *Johns Hopkins Magazine,* Vol. 24 XXIV, No. 2, May 1973.

93. Interview with James D. Watson, "Children from the Laboratory," *Prism,* Vol. 1, No. 2, May 1973.

94. *Human Life Review,* Vol. I, No. 3 (Summer, 1975), p. 98.

95. P. Ramsey, *The Ethics of Fetal Research* (New Haven, Conn.: Yale University Press, 1975).

96. *Federal Register,* Vol. 50 #154, p. 33520, August 8, 1975.

97. H. O. J. Brown, "Fetal Research II, The Ethical Question," *Human Life Review,* Vol. I, No. 4, p. 121, 1975.

98. *Medical Tribune,* October 24, 1973.

99. K. M. Mitzner, "The Growing Scandal of Abortion," *Christianity Applied,* November 1974.

100. Newsletter of Americans United for Life, Vol. 1, No. 2, January 1973.

101. Wilson, E. O., et al, *Life on Earth* (Stamford, Conn.: Sinauer Assoc. Inc., 1973).

102. P. and A. Ehrlich, *Human Ecology, Problems and Solutions* (San Francisco: W. H. Freeman, 1973).

103. B. Nathanson, "Ambulatory Abortions, Experience with 26,000 Cases, July 1970—August 1971," *New England Journal of Medicine,* 286-403, 1972.

104. B. Nathanson, "Deeper into Abortion," *New England Journal of Medicine,* 1189, 1974.

105. "Burden of Guilt," New York *Times* News Service in the *Evening Gazette,* Worcester, Mass., June 4, 1975.

106. Physicians International Press, quoted in Newsletter of

Americans United for Life, Vol. II, No. 2, June 1975.

107. *Boston Pilot, N. C. News,* Feb. 2, 1974.

108. *Constitutional Right to Live* v. *Joseph E. Cannan et al,* C. A. 374-194 (Rhode Island).

109. Interim Report, Americans United for Life, Dec. 23, 1975.

110. Joseph O'Meara, "Abortion: The Court Decides a Non-Case," *Human Life Review,* Vol. I, No. 4, 1975.

111. Malcolm Muggeridge, "What the Abortion Argument Is About," *Human Life Review,* Vol. I, No. 3, 1975.

CHAPTER 2

1. Declaration of Independence.

2. 2 Corinthians 5:8.

3. R. S. Duff and A. G. M. Campbell, "Moral and Ethical Dilemmas in the Special Care Nursery," *New England Journal of Medicine* 289:890, 1973.

4. *Medical World News,* May 5, 1974.

5. *Human Life Review,* Vol. I, No. 3, p. 76.

6. *Human Life Review,* Vol. I, No. 3, p. 76.

7. *Time* Magazine, November 3, 1975, p. 52.

8. *Time,* Nov. 3, 1975, p. 52.

9. *Time,* Nov. 3, 1975, p. 52.

10. *Time,* Nov. 3, 1975, p. 58.

11. *Sunday Times Advertiser,* Trenton, N. J., November 2, 1975.

12. Paul Ramsey, "The Indignity of Death with Dignity," *Hastings Center Study,* May, 1974.

13. *Time,* November 24, 1975, p. 70.

14. Editorial, Philadelphia *Inquirer,* November 12, 1975. William A. Reusher, Op-Ed page, Philadelphia *Inquirer,* November 23, 1975.

15. See Note 14.

16. Isaiah 14:14.